STARS

STARS

REFLECTIONS ON CHRISTMAS BY

Chieko N. Okazaki

DESERET
BOOK

SALT LAKE CITY, UTAH

Poem on page 35 by Marian Wright Edelman. Reprinted by permission of the Children's Defense Fund, 25 E Street, NW, Washington, D.C. 20001. www.childrensdefense.org. All rights reserved.

Story on pages 47–49 from "Christmas Day in the Morning," by Pearl S. Buck. Reprinted by permission of Harold Ober Associates Incorporated. Copyright © 1955 by Pearl S. Buck. Copyright renewed 1983.

Story on pages 99–101 from "Christmas in Dixie," by Lyda Jean Bennett. Reprinted with permission from Guideposts. Copyright © 1995 by Guideposts, Carmel, New York 10512. All rights reserved.

Story on pages 103–8 from "An Exchange of Gifts," by Diane Rayner. Reprinted with permission from Guideposts. Copyright © 1987 by Guideposts, Carmel, New York 10512. All rights reserved.

Poem on pages 115–16 by Jean de Brébeuf; translated by Jesse Edgar Middleton. Reprinted by permission of Frederick Harris Music, 2250 Military Rd., Tonawanda, New York 14150. All rights reserved.

Story on pages 133–37 from "The Secret of Our Survival," by James E. Ray. Reprinted with permission from Guideposts. Copyright © 1996 by Guideposts, Carmel, New York 10512. All rights reserved.

We acknowledge copyright holders whose material may be included but whom we were unable to contact. If any acknowledgments have been overlooked, please notify the publisher, and omissions will be rectified in future editions.

Library of Congress Cataloging-in-Publication Data

Okazaki, Chieko N., 1926-
  Stars / Chieko Okazaki.
    p. cm.
  Includes bibliographical references.
  ISBN 1-59038-353-2 (hardcover : alk. paper)
  1. Christmas. 2. Christian life—Mormon authors. I. Title.
  BV45.O53 2004
  242'.335—dc22

2004010524

Printed in the United States of America   72076
Publishers Printing, Salt Lake City, Utah

10   9   8   7   6   5   4   3   2   1

CONTENTS

1

Star Without,
Star Within

The blessed Christmas season turns our hearts in wonder and joy to the steadfast love of the Savior for each one of us. We are also reminded of the love of our Heavenly Parents, who seek our eternal progression and who hold back nothing from the goal of increasing our opportunities to grow spiritually—no, nothing was withheld, not even the life of their cherished and beloved son, Jesus Christ.

The glorious music of Christmas reminds us of the miracle of God himself being born as a baby among us to succor us in our need and to save us from death and sin and despair. It increases my thanksgiving. It increases my joy. It increases the blessedness of this time.

I remember a program on PBS a few years ago in which Carl Sagan was explaining how the universe came into being. The idea that impressed me the most was his description of how the Big Bang blew billions of tons of particulate matter to all corners of the universe—dust, if you want to call it that. Star dust. These bits of dust travel on cosmic winds and eddy around our planet. Tons have fallen to earth to mingle with the soil that itself developed through many stages from that primordial matter. Then—and this was the exciting part for me—Carl Sagan went a step further and told how this dust from the stars has become part of the food we eat and the water we drink, part of our cells, part of our beings.

How does that make you feel, to know you carry part of the stars themselves from the very dawn of creation within you? It's another way of looking at the concept we already know from the scriptures: that there is no such thing as immaterial matter; that the light of Christ fills the immensity of space, making each part of the universe related to every other part; and that we are eternal in our essence. Truly we live and move and have our beings within the miraculous.

I want to share some thoughts about stars, the stars without and the stars within—not just the star-stuff that is part of the genetic inheritance of our bodies, but also the star that comes from a spiritual knowing of who we are, of feeling that eternal light burning steadily as a thousand suns within us. It is the feeling Amos captures in this wonderful phrase, "the star of your god." (Amos 5:26.)

I'd like us to begin by recalling a story from the scriptures. The story of the wise men from Matthew 2 is probably familiar to you—one you have heard and loved since childhood.

Now when Jesus was born in Bethlehem of Judaea in the days of Herod the king, behold, there came wise men from the east to Jerusalem,

Saying, Where is he that is born King of the Jews? for we have seen his star in the east, and are come to worship him.

When Herod the king had heard these things, he was troubled, and all Jerusalem with him.

And when he had gathered all the chief priests and scribes of the people together, he demanded of them where Christ should be born.

And they said unto him, In Bethlehem of Judaea: for thus it is written by the prophet,

And thou Bethlehem, in the land of Juda, art not the least among the princes of Juda: for out of thee shall come a Governor, that shall rule my people Israel.

Then Herod, when he had privily called the wise men, enquired of them diligently what time the star appeared.

And he sent them to Bethlehem, and said, Go and search diligently for the young child; and when ye have found him, bring me word again, that I may come and worship him also.

When they had heard the king, they departed; and, lo, the star, which they saw in the east, went before them, till it came and stood over where the young child was. (Matthew 2:1–9.)

We know very little of the wise men, although some lovely thoughts, hymns, legends, and stories have grown up to fill the gaps in our knowledge with inspirational and adventuresome ideas about them. And I certainly have no new sources of information to add about them. Likewise, we do not know what, in astronomical terms, caused the star, whether it was a conjunction of planets, a supernova whose light just then reached the earth, or something else. But it doesn't really matter.

We think of the star of Bethlehem, the star that the wise men followed so patiently and so hopefully and so faithfully, as a phenomenon in the heavens, and so it was. But I tell you that the star in the heavens was not the only star or the most important star. The star within the heart of the wise men was the important star. After all, if the star was in the sky for all to see, then hundreds of thousands of people would have seen it and thousands of people could have wondered at its meaning, and hundreds could have followed it to the little town of Bethlehem. But as far as we know, only the wise men saw it with the eye of faith. Only they followed it with hope and patience. Only they kneeled before the young child, Jesus. *They had a star within that enabled them to see the star without.* They saw it with the eyes of faith, and it brought them to Jesus.

We don't know what happened to the star. The last mention is that it "stood" over the place where they found Jesus. Presumably it disappeared afterward, its work accomplished, but we don't know that. Nor do we know where the wise men went after they bestowed their gifts, worshiped the child, and took their leave.

What I think we can say with some assurance is that they took the star away with them—the star that really counted, the star within. That star did not depend on human sight or on a phenomenon in the heavens or the machinations of kings and rulers.

The Star Within

First, let's consider the star within. I want to tell you a story that moved me greatly when I heard it at a BYU Women's Conference. Marti Holloman's husband worked at the American embassy in Beijing, while Marti coped with the challenges of raising three children in China. One of the people she met exemplifies the trait of carrying a star within. He was a gifted artist named Wang whom Marti and her husband met at an art exhibit one December. This is the story she tells.

> [Wang] inquired where my husband learned his Chinese. "You were a missionary?" he said with whispered excitement. Quietly he told us he had learned his English from American Protestant missionaries some forty years earlier. Because his family members were Christians and wealthy landowners, they suffered at the hands of the Communist revolutionaries. His father died, the family lost their home and their money, buried their Bibles, and kept their faith safe in their hearts. His dream of attending a university to study art was short-lived. During the Cultural Revolution, he was expelled and eventually imprisoned for being both religious and an intellectual. Yet throughout this ordeal, his faith never wavered.
>
> Hearing his story, my husband felt impressed to invite him to a caroling party we were hosting. It was part of a cultural exchange with the Chinese university at which my husband studied and we both taught. This exchange

occurred only because we were there during a rare window of time when there was far greater openness to Western ideas than in the past.

The previous year our lecture on Western Christmas traditions at the university drew standing-room-only crowds—with our middle-aged students dancing afterwards with wreaths around their necks and garlands on their heads, declaring that the next week they would have a university Christmas party in the lecture hall. They felt the infectious joy of the season. The school cook made two cakes that said "Christmas Happy," we had an obligatory power failure, and by candlelight Santa Holloman came "ni hao-hao-hao-ing" into pandemonium. So, by this, the second year, we were inundated with requests to produce multiple university celebrations to accommodate all the new Christmas enthusiasts.

With that precedent and the administration's blessing, we welcomed Wang and a huge crowd of students into our home on Christmas Eve to have cookies and cider, see their first Christmas tree and stockings, and to sing carols in the neighborhood (rehearsed as part of our English lesson). Santa Holloman led the band of carolers through the streets on that starry Christmas Eve. They sang by candlelight and delivered plates of cookies to . . . bewildered but delighted neighbors, workmen, and soldiers.

In the midst of all the faces struggling to read the unfamiliar songs, we saw our new friend, Wang, his head held high, singing the carols from memory and with such exuberance that he captured the hearts of all the carolers. When the party was over, he lingered. He had brought gifts for each one of us—the finest treasures from his art exhibit. These were true gifts from the heart. He felt such joy in giving them, yet they surely represented many months' wages for him. What made us feel worse was that in the midst of all the preparations we had forgotten he was coming and had no gift for him! But the Lord, in his perfect timing, had seen to it that my brother's gift to us arrived that very day: a Metropolitan Museum of Art book entitled *Christmas by the Great Masters*. It was the perfect gift for an artist, and as we presented it to him, Wang explained that he hadn't seen such paintings since his childhood. "Da-vinsky!" "Oh, Michelangelo!" "Oh, so beautiful!" he exclaimed as he looked at the paintings of the Nativity that had once been banned.

With great enthusiasm, he asked, "Could we please sing more carols?" So we gathered by the tree and sang. Then he turned to my husband and said, "Mr. Holloman, would you please tell the Christmas story?" That request presented us with a dilemma: we were allowed to worship in the privacy of our own home but were strictly forbidden to proselyte (a law we steadfastly honored). We were allowed to share Christmas traditions with our students, but we were not to talk about their religious implications, other than a cursory mention that the season did commemorate the birth of Jesus Christ.

No, it was, after all, Christmas Eve, and every year of our lives we had read the Christmas story on Christmas Eve—it was part of our culture. And here was this earnest request before us. It was nearly midnight, and our children were waiting. My husband drew a breath and began reading the familiar words from Luke. We looked at our friend and realized that he was silently mouthing the words he had committed to memory as a child so many years before. "Please, more carols!" he said, and we sang and sang, ending with "Silent Night." The lights of the Christmas tree reflected tears in our friend's eyes, and as he stood to leave, he said, "Oh, thank you! Thank you! This is the first Christmas I've had in thirty-six years."[1]

Could you be faithful that long? I'm seventy-eight. Thirty-six is a little less than half of my lifetime. I ask myself if I could have been faithful, keeping the words of the Christmas story and the words of the Christmas carols in my heart for half a lifetime. Wang could. He carried them like a star within.

We do not know when our lives will require that we, like the wise men, set off on a long pilgrimage, the end of which we cannot see. Will we have a star to guide us? We do not know when the stars in our personal sky will go out, leaving us in darkness. At that point, will we have a star within to guide us? Jesus warned that before his second coming "the sun [would] be darkened, and the moon shall not give her light, and the stars shall fall from heaven." (Matthew 24:29.) Will a star within give us a bright and steady light in that turmoil and darkness?

I give you a Christmas invitation to set some stars in your personal sky. Perhaps I was greatly influenced by Sister Holloman's story of Wang, but I would like this invitation to focus your thoughts on beautiful and powerful scriptures, poems, or other expressions that can be part of your personal firmament, reminding you that God is in his heaven and giving you comfort for times of loneliness, words to express your joy at times of happiness, glorious words with which to express your faith.

You know that I used to teach elementary schoolchildren. So it shouldn't surprise you that I like to use a visual aid to help me remember these personal stars. Do you recall the kind of star that you used to get in Primary if you had said the prayer or participated in sharing time or were especially good in class? I think it's a good idea to have one of those stars and to put it somewhere you'll notice.

You can put it on your forehead if you want. I put mine on my watch. That way I'll remember, every time I look at my watch, that there's time in my day to think about Jesus, to feel his love for me, to express my gratitude for him, and to think about the star within that glows because he is the light of the world. It can be a reminder to find a lovely passage of scripture to inspire you, or it can be a reminder to ponder the passage you have chosen and to let those living words sink deep into your heart.

While I was preparing this chapter, I came across some beautiful scriptures about stars—scriptures that brought peace and rejoicing, and an outpouring of gratitude to our wonderful God. Here is the testimony of Balaam, a prophet who was not even an Israelite, testifying of God:

> I shall see him, but not now: I shall behold him, but not nigh: there shall come a Star out of Jacob, and a Sceptre shall rise out of Israel, and . . . out of Jacob shall come he that shall have dominion. (Numbers 24:17, 19.)

There is the glorious anthem of praise in God's magnificent questioning of Job:

> Where wast thou when I laid the foundations of the earth? declare, if thou hast understanding.
>
> Who hath laid the measures thereof, if thou knowest? or who hath stretched the line upon it?
>
> Whereupon are the foundations thereof fastened? or who laid the corner stone thereof;
>
> When the morning stars sang together, and all the sons of God shouted for joy? (Job 38:4–7.)

The Psalms express the same sense of exaltation:

> When I consider thy heavens, the work of thy fingers, the moon and the stars, which thou hast ordained;
>
> What is man, that thou art mindful of him? and the son of man, that thou visitest him?
>
> For thou hast made him a little lower than the angels, and hast crowned him with glory and honour.
>
> Thou madest him to have dominion over the works of thy hands; thou hast put all things under his feet:
>
> All sheep and oxen, yea, and the beasts of the field;
>
> The fowl of the air, and the fish of the sea, and whatsoever passeth through the paths of the seas.
>
> O Lord our Lord, how excellent is thy name in all the earth! (Psalm 8:3–9.)
>
> Praise ye the Lord: for it is good to sing praises unto our God; . . .

The Lord doth build up Jerusalem: he gathereth
together the outcasts of Israel.

He healeth the broken in heart, and bindeth up their
wounds.

He telleth the number of the stars; he calleth them all
by their names.

Great is our Lord, and of great power: his understanding is infinite. (Psalm 147:1–5.)

And here is one from Amos, the shepherd prophet, who
knew the creations of God from his hours of intimate observa-
tions during the dawns and dusks of a shepherd's life:

Seek him that maketh the seven stars and Orion, and
turneth the shadow of death into the morning, and maketh
the day dark with night: that calleth for the waters of the
sea, and poureth them out upon the face of the earth: The
Lord is his name. (Amos 5:8.)

Those are some of the scriptural stars in my sky. I invite you
to find just one scripture or poem or hymn text that can be a star
in your personal sky, a star within, for you during this Christmas
season, something to meditate on, to find wonder in, to thank God
for, and to find increased beauty in. If you can, the meaning of that
scripture or thought will unfold to you like the petals of a rose. It
will be a small but steady light for you in this month of December.

The Star Without

But what about the star without—the external star? Please
think with me about that star. It led the wise men from a starting

point we do not know except that it was in the east. It led them across distances we cannot imagine. It seems to have deserted them momentarily so that they had to go to King Herod's court to seek direction. Or perhaps they felt that they had surely reached their destination and confidently went to the place where they expected to find the newborn king. But they were looking in the wrong place.

The king's wise men had the books and records. They read the scripture saying that the child would be born in Bethlehem. But they were no good as guides. None of them had gone to Bethlehem looking for a baby. No, they all stayed safely in their comfort zones with their books and charts and knowledge.

The wise men had faith in their words—more faith than Herod's chief priests and scribes. They set out for Bethlehem. Then, the scripture says:

> They departed; and lo, the star, which they saw in the east, went before them, till it came and stood over where the young child was.
>
> When they saw the star, they rejoiced with exceeding great joy. (Matthew 2:9–10.)

The point I want to make is that they had to leave the palace before they saw the star again and before they received any guidance from it. There is no suggestion that the chief priests and the scribes were evil or even that they lacked understanding, but it is clear that they could only talk about the king. They did not know him. They did not seek him. And—I hope you did not miss this point—they did not find him.

What is the lesson for us in this part of the Christmas story? It is not enough for us to know what the scriptures say. It is not enough for us to have knowledge—even correct and complete knowledge. We will not see the star unless we leave the court. We will not be led unless we are willing to move. We will not find the child unless we are willing to journey to a place that may only be a strange and foreign name on our mental map. And we will never know what it feels like to "rejoice with exceeding great joy" unless we yearn and seek and journey.

And what happened next? The star confirmed the dwelling place of the baby—no longer an infant but a young child, and no longer in a stable but in a house:

> And when they were come into the house, they saw the young child with Mary his mother, and fell down, and worshipped him: and when they had opened their treasures, they presented unto him gifts; gold, and frankincense, and myrrh. (Matthew 2:11.)

Let me pick out two ideas to develop just for a moment. The first is that they immediately recognized that Jesus was the child they were looking for. How did they recognize him? We don't know. He was a Jewish youngster less than two years old. He may have been so young that he couldn't even walk yet. He may have been old enough to be at that exhilarating, wonderful baby stage when he knows how to toddle across the room to his mother's arms. He might have been able to say a few words. But they knew him. Somehow they knew him, and they worshiped him.

They recognized divinity in this ordinary, dark-haired little boy. That's a challenge for us, too. If we let the star lead us to a strange place with a mysterious name that is not our home, will we be able to recognize the divinity in the person we find there? I suggest that if we can enter with reverence into the heart-space made by other human beings and offer them our recognition of their personhood and our respectful presence, we will know how the wise men recognized the Lord of all the earth in that little dark-eyed boy.

Let the star lead you to a stranger to whom you can offer a respectful presence, in whom you can see the eternal and immortal soul who is your brother or your sister. I remember a story told by Elder Marion D. Hanks about how

> . . . the windows of a great department store in New York City are used to express a special idea each year at Christmas time. In these windows there are pictured the affluent, the happy homes at Christmas, and the bridge abutment under which the hobos are gathered to cook a meal in a tin can. There are pictured the joyous, happy children, and there is the sick person in bed, and the woman with a baby, her face pressed to the window. And there is one message, "If Christ came tonight, to whom would he come?"[2]

If we are wise, we will not look for the divine child in the courts of a king. We will let the star lead us to the stranger. This stranger may be someone you sit next to on the bus for ten minutes. This stranger may be the person who has been in the office next to you for ten years but whose story you have never asked to know and whose spirit you have not yet engaged with reverence and love. This person may be someone in your family whose material needs are met but whose heart is still hungry. So first, let the star lead you to a stranger.

The second idea is that the wise men had something to give this child. They came prepared with gifts, and these gifts were acceptable. You may not know what gifts you have available to give until you see the need. It is popular in our culture to decry materialism, but there are many spiritual needs that cannot be addressed until someone is no longer hungry or cold or in pain from an unaddressed medical need. There is a reason why gold is an acceptable gift.

As for frankincense and myrrh, these are perfumes, aromatic spices that had a role in worship at the time. We can see immediately how gold—or money, or the goods and services money can buy—can be a great gift in our own time. But perhaps frankincense and myrrh may not seem so directly applicable as gold.

Actually, I like the fact that we can't instantly make a one-to-one correlation, because that leaves us free to imagine, to dream, to let the connections emerge for us out of our own experience. What might such a gift be that would let you communicate rejoicing and reverence and love? Could a plate of cookies for a neighbor be frankincense? Might an hour learning a new song with your preschooler be myrrh? Who knows? You get to decide. You get to choose. You get to make something wonderful.

As I've thought about the way an aromatic perfume wafts through the rooms of a house, I think of the spicy aftershave my husband used to wear. Christmas was Ed's favorite time of year.

He was a generous, loving individual all year round, but he was in the height of his glory at Christmastime.

When I was first called to the Relief Society general presidency, Ed did everything he could to support me. He took over the laundry and much of the cleaning. He took telephone messages and ran errands, and took clothes to the dry cleaners and picked them up. He handled the bills, changed the furnace filter, and put new salt in the water softener—everything he could think of to save time for me. Every time he read a magazine, he'd clip or mark the articles that he thought I could use and even went through back issues looking for material. This is one of the stories he found, written maybe twenty years ago by Lew Barry:

> On a cold, blustery, winter day in Denver, I witnessed a heartwarming tableau. At a street crossing, a Spanish-American girl about 11 years old, was buttoning her own coat around a much smaller girl, probably her little sister. The older girl now faced the wintry wind clad in a flimsy dress.
>
> Just then the driver of the car ahead of me slammed on his brakes, and a young man got out and went over to the girls, taking off a good-looking tweed topcoat as he went. Folding the coat around the older sister, he patted her awkwardly on the shoulder, then quickly got back into his car and drove away.

I love this story for three reasons: first, because we used to live in Denver; second, because even though the man who gave his coat wasn't Ed, that's exactly the kind of thing Ed would do. In fact, I've seen him leave the homeless shelter in his shirtsleeves because he'd literally given someone the coat off his back. And third, because I feel so appreciative to this man, Lew Barry, for having been the witness to a double act of spontaneous generosity that is ennobling to read about and for having taken the time to share it. The chances are small that I will ever meet Lew Barry in this life, but he has brightened and bettered my life by his tribute to a loving big sister and a passing stranger, neither of whom he knew.

And now I've told the story to you. Maybe twenty years from now, it will still be brightening your heart to know there is such nobility of character, such spontaneous generosity among this species we call human beings. These are experiences that can happen when we let a star lead us.

These thoughts are just my own ideas without any scriptural foundation, but I have thought how many beautiful things would happen if we would search, not in likely places but in unlikely ones, for an uncrowned king, unrecognizable except to the eyes of faith, and if we had gifts to give.

Will you let a star lead you this Christmas season to an unusual place—not, perhaps, one that you would choose yourself? Will you look at the stranger you find in that place and see holiness in his or her face?

Conclusion

Now, it is Christmastime. Christ waits to be born anew in our hearts as he does each Christmas season. His star is in the heavens, and wise men and wise women seek him still. And the starlight they follow and the starlight they carry away with him in their hearts are both real.

Contemplate the star without. Let it lead you to a stable or a simple house where someone needs the touch of your hand, your presence that acknowledges and respects the divinity present in each person, where your gifts of gold and frankincense and myrrh will make a difference.

Then contemplate the star within. Let the light that recognizes your yearning and your desire to serve flood your heart so that it radiates from your very countenance. Recognize that you have star material within you—no, something more precious and important than star-stuff. You have God-material within you, the essence of the divine nature. Let that star be a light for you in the throne rooms of the Herods you must confront. Let it show you the faces of the angels who come into your life to warn you to take another way home. And as you take those other paths, know that the light goes with you.

Each Christmas season, we hear the angels' song of "Glory to God! Glory in the highest!" Let me close with the exultant words of Joseph Smith, who praised God in a passage that rivals the angels' song for beauty:

> How glorious is the voice we hear from heaven, proclaiming in our ears, glory, and salvation, and honor, and immortality, and eternal life; kingdoms, principalities, and powers! . . . Let the mountains shout for joy, and all ye valleys cry aloud; and all ye seas and dry lands tell the wonders of your Eternal King! And ye rivers, and brooks, and rills, flow down with gladness. Let the woods and all the

trees of the field praise the Lord; and ye solid rocks weep for joy! And let the sun, moon, and the morning stars sing together, and let all the [children] of God shout for joy! And let the eternal creations declare his name forever and ever! (D&C 128:23.)

May the joy of Christmas glow in your heart like the light of an eternal star.

NOTES

1. Marti Holloman and Marcie Holloman, "Right Person, Right Place, Right Time," in *Clothed with Charity: Talks from the 1996 Women's Conference,* edited by Dawn Hall Anderson, Susette Fletcher Green, and Dlora Hall Dalton (Salt Lake City: Deseret Book, 1997), 225–28.
2. Marion D. Hanks, "Was He Relevant?" *Speeches of the Year* pamphlet [Provo: BYU Press, December 17, 1968], 10.

2

SEEKING THE CHILD

During this beautiful season of Christmas, I would like to share with you some thoughts about its promise, its hope, and its joy. I would like to renew with you President Howard W. Hunter's invitation to us all "to live with ever more attention to the life and example of the Lord Jesus Christ, especially the love and hope and compassion He displayed."[1]

One of my favorite stories about President Hunter occurred on his eightieth birthday. His family congregated at his home, and his two daughters-in-law set his dining room table with elegant china, crystal, and silver.

> After dinner the family sat around the table and took turns telling [President Hunter] what they most admired about him and how he had influenced their lives. It was, according to [one of his daughters-in-law], a tender time,

with many tears shed. Then someone said, "Tell us, Grandpa, what you think we should know—what advice do you have for our lives." After a brief pause, . . . [President Hunter] replied solemnly, "Well, when you take a shower, keep the curtains inside the tub."[2]

Well, I have a few words of advice that may apply to the Christmas season too. I hope it's as practical and applicable as President Hunter's to his grandchildren.

I've titled this chapter "Seeking the Child." I want to look at three journeys to seek the babe of Bethlehem and how each one might apply in our lives. You're familiar with all three, I'm sure, because they're from the scriptures. But rather than read the accounts from the New Testament as they appear in the beautiful, stately language of the King James translation, I want to just tell you the story in simple, ordinary speech, as though I had heard this amazing story from a friend and was passing it on to you because it was so interesting and so thrilling. What if it was true—the angels and the baby and the strangers from the east? Can you read as though you were hearing it for the first time?

The Journey of the Shepherds

The first journey I want to tell you about is the journey of the shepherds who were spending the night in the fields outside Bethlehem, taking care of their flocks.

An angel of the Lord appeared to them, and the glory of the Lord shone over them. They were terribly afraid, but the angel said to them, "Don't be afraid! For I am here with good news for you, which will bring great joy to all the people. This very night in David's town, your Savior was born—Christ the Lord! This is what will prove it to you: you will find a baby wrapped in cloths and lying in a manger."

Suddenly a great army of heaven's angels appeared with the angel, singing praises to God: "Glory to God in the highest heaven! And peace to those on earth whose hearts are filled with good will."

When the angels went away from them back into heaven, the shepherds said one to another, "Let us go to Bethlehem and see this thing that has happened, that the Lord has told us."

So they hurried off and found Mary and Joseph and saw the baby lying in the manger. They told Mary and Joseph what the angel had said about this child, and all who heard it were filled with wonder. Then the shepherds went back, singing praises to God for all they had heard and seen. It had been just as the angel had told them. (Luke 2:8–20.)

Think about the shepherds' journey to seek the child. Each one of us lives in a world that demands work and has bills that come due. Yet each of us has journeys that take us to spiritual experiences, to experiences of testimony and faith and new understandings.

But the point I want to make is that the message came to the shepherds—not because they were waiting for it or because they were seeking it—but simply because they were going about their normal workaday occupations. This glorious and blessed experience broke in upon them and chose them. For a few hours it made their lives extraordinary. And then they returned to their workaday occupations.

I often wonder what happened to the shepherds for the next thirty years while Jesus was growing up. These shepherds were probably the fathers and older brothers of the babies who were later slain by Herod's soldiers. Did they have trouble reconciling the message of the angel with the death that visited their homes two years later? Were any of them still alive in thirty years when Jesus began his ministry, and did they recognize in the prince of peace that tiny baby they had worshiped? We just don't know the answer to those questions.

But I think that Christmas comes to us in the hustle and bustle of our workaday worlds and, if we are willing to hear the angel, we can be lifted out of our humdrum existence for a few glorious hours that will bring us to the manger of the Christ child. Then when we return to our ordinary worlds, we have the memory of something shining and beautiful.

Yet Christmas—this extraordinary and shining gift—can become just another part of our busy, bustling schedules. We can secularize Christmas even while we think we are celebrating it. I want to explore this idea in very personal terms, because I have celebrated Christmas as a Buddhist, when it was a warm and friendly holiday but a completely secular one, and I have also celebrated it as a Christian, filled with the reverence and awe of knowing that the Son of God had himself come down to be a helpless baby and to share mortality with us so that he could lift and lead and redeem us.

When I was growing up as a Buddhist child on the big

island of Hawaii, I knew what Christmas was, of course, because it was an important part of our local festivities. Captain Beck was the manager of the local sugar-cane plantation where everybody in my little village of Mahukona worked. And every year, he and his wife would host a Christmas pageant, with caroling, good food, and a half-scary but thrilling visit from a strange fat man with white whiskers and a red suit of clothes who shouted "Ho, ho, ho!" very loudly and passed out sacks of candy. One year I was the angel who announced the "glad tidings" in a costume made of a sheet and a crooked halo made of tinsel.

When I started school, every December we would color Christmas trees and learn to sing Christmas carols about children who were naughty or nice and about a little town called Bethlehem. (This was back in the days when Buddhists didn't think they were imposed upon to learn Christian songs and when Christians didn't think they were being cultural imperialists to share their favorite holiday of the year with Buddhists.) We would have a Christmas tree at the school and a Christmas party.

Later, when I returned from college, my mother and father had adopted Christmas customs for my three younger brothers with a lighted and decorated tree, presents, and parties at the school and in the neighborhood. There was no sense of religion—no mention of Jesus and no mention of Santa Claus, either. It was just a holiday—a happy time of family and neighborly togetherness, but with no sense of religious awe or the feeling that it was a pivotal moment in the year.

Instead, it became a sort of prelude to our Japanese New

Year's celebration, which involved sweeping the house from top to bottom on the day of New Year's Eve and cooking dozens of dishes. On New Year's Eve, we kept the doors and windows open, a folk custom that was supposed to let out the evil spirits from the previous year, and everybody got to stay up until midnight. Our dear Hawaiian neighbors, who were not Japanese, participated just as willingly in our celebration as we participated in their Christian celebration, and they came from house to house like carolers singing love songs and popular songs in their rich, harmonizing voices. What any of this had to do with New Year's was pretty vague, but what was concrete was the feeling of joy and love they brought with them. They sang from the heart, accompanying themselves on ukuleles and other instruments and sampling our Japanese specialties before going on to the next house.

On New Year's Day, we laid out a buffet and spent the day receiving guests and also going from house to house ourselves, extending and receiving good wishes for the New Year and sampling a wonderful range of goodies.

We still did all of these things after I joined the Church at the age of fifteen, but everything was different because now I understood about that baby! I understood the miracle of that baby who was born poor and homeless but our Lord and King. My youngest brother, David, was born the year I went away to college. I thought about what it meant to be a newborn child, helpless and dependent. I thought about the trust that Jesus had in Mary in agreeing to become her son, the love that Mary had for Jesus in accepting the responsibilities of motherhood, the trust of the Lord in Joseph to share his son with them.

I remember walking to the branch at Halaula, where I went to church all the time I was going to high school after I was baptized. It was closer than my home branch of Mahukona, but it was still about ten miles away. I would pick up Lily Higa, a girl a year or so younger who lived on the way, and we would walk together. Most days we were lucky and someone would give us a ride. When it rained, we'd take off our shoes and walk barefoot, then wash our feet when we got to church, pop our shoes back on, and go in to our meetings. I hadn't seen Lily since 1948, but I saw her recently in Chicago. Her husband had died and she was serving a mission there, and I recognized her at once when she came to a conference where I spoke. If you don't think that was a Christmas feeling!

We had learned all of the Christmas songs like "Silent Night" and "O Little Town of Bethlehem" at school, and we loved singing them at church, too, but my favorite Christmas song was "Far, Far Away on Judea's Plains." It was one we never learned at school, and I was very proud when I learned that it had been written by a Latter-day Saint. It's still my favorite Christmas carol. I really enjoy requesting "Far, Far Away on Judea's Plains" as a rest song when I have a speaking assignment—not only because I enjoy the song but also because I enjoy the startled looks on people's faces when I ask for this song in the middle of August.

> *Far, far away on Judea's plains,*
> *Shepherds of old heard the joyous strains:*

Glory to God, Glory to God, Glory to God in the
> *highest;*
Peace on earth, goodwill to men;
Peace on earth, goodwill to men!

Whenever I hear that song, it makes me remember what it feels like to be lifted out of our everyday existence for a few glorious moments. Let's each take the shepherds' journey this Christmas—a journey of eager faith, a journey of worship, a journey of joy.

The Journey of the Wise Men

This brings us to the second journey to seek the child. This is the journey of the wise men. Again, read this story as if you were hearing it for the first time in the ordinary speech you would use to talk about some out-of-town visitors who had come to the neighbors a few houses down:

> Soon after Jesus was born, some men who studied the stars came from the east to Jerusalem and asked, "Where is the baby born to be the king of the Jews? We saw his star when it came up in the east, and we have come to worship him."
>
> When King Herod heard about this, he was very upset, and so was everybody else in Jerusalem. He called together all the chief priests and teachers of the Law and asked them, "Where will the Messiah be born?" "In the town of Bethlehem, in Judea," they answered. This is what the prophet wrote: "You, Bethlehem, in the land of Judah, are not by any means the least among the rulers of Judah;

for from you will come a leader who will guide my people Israel."

So Herod called the visitors from the east to a secret meeting and found out from them the exact time the star had appeared. Then he sent them to Bethlehem with these instructions: "Go and make a careful search for the child, and when you find him let me know, so that I may go and worship him too."

With this, they left, and on their way they saw the star—the same one they had seen in the east—and it went ahead of them until it came and stopped over the place where the child was. How happy they were, and what gladness they felt when they saw the star!

They went into the house and saw the child with his mother, Mary. They knelt down and worshiped him; then they opened their bags and offered him presents: gold, frankincense, and myrrh. (Matthew 2:1–11.)

Unlike the shepherds, the wise men were strangers. They didn't know the fields and streets of Bethlehem; they didn't even know where Bethlehem was. While the shepherds came with faith that what the angel had told them was true, the wise men traveled from afar, moving for many days. They came with faith, leaving their own people, their own languages, their own country to enter a dangerous country, to seek advice from strangers who tried to exploit their knowledge, and then had to return a different way than they had come.

Let me compare the hope of the wise men to my experiences of celebrating Christmas as a stranger who was welcomed into the homes of others who had enough Christmas spirit to share with me and with my family.

I think of Kenneth and Jean Springer, dear members of the Presbyterian Church, who lived just two or three houses away from our little basement apartment in Salt Lake City. I had taught their daughter, Susan, in my second-grade class, and they had simply swept Ed, Ken, Bob, and me under their wings. They were so unfailingly kind to us, and such beautiful people. Ken, our oldest son, is named for Ken Springer.

We were frequently guests in their home, but when Ken was two, I'll always remember, they invited us to Christmas dinner. It was a gorgeous meal on a beautiful table: turkey, mashed potatoes and gravy, dressing, several kinds of vegetables and salads, and Jean's delicious mincemeat pie and pumpkin pie. Ken surveyed all of this bounteous and beautiful food and then started to cry. He sat on his chair trying to behave well, but big tears were just rolling down his face.

Aunt Jeannie asked, "Why are you crying, Ken?"

And he sobbed, "You don't have any rice. You just have mashed potatoes."

So Ed and I had to explain, "When Uncle Ken and Aunt Jeannie come to our house, we have rice, because that's what I cook. When we go to Uncle Ken and Aunt Jeannie's, we have mashed potatoes, because that's what Aunt Jeannie cooks. That's fair, isn't it?"

And Ken very maturely admitted that it was fair and graciously ate his mashed potatoes. But what I remember is the kindness of the Springers to this little stranger in their midst who was homesick for rice. They were kind to all of us. We were all homesick, trying to have Mormon Christmases in a place where the ground was covered with snow and the air hurt if you breathed too deeply. It didn't matter to the Springers that we were Japanese, that we were Hawaiians, and that we were Mormons. We were strangers who had come from afar, and their home was open to us.

I have always remembered this and tried to be sensitive to other strangers in our midst who may be secretly weeping over the equivalent of mashed potatoes while they are homesick for rice. I loved our wards in Denver. Almost no one had extended families there in the wards, so the ward itself became an extended family, and we shared holidays and treats with each other just as we shared our faith and testimonies and our appreciation for each other.

Will you remember the journey of the wise men to seek the child? There are times and situations and circumstances in our lives when a shepherd's response of a few hours or an interrupted night's sleep is not enough. To set our lives in order or to gain the kind of living faith in the Savior that we must have, we may need to make the journey of the wise men, leaving our psychological homes and familiar surroundings, testing the flattering words of the Herods who surround us, being willing to travel far with only the glimmer of a star to guide us. We must travel sometimes with only hope as our companion, because we saw no angels and heard no majestic choirs singing. But hope is enough to lead us to the Savior if we will persevere.

A wise man of our own day, our beloved prophet, President Gordon B. Hinckley, has said:

> When all is said and done, . . . when all of history is examined, when the deepest depths of the human mind have been explored, there is nothing so wonderful, so majestic, so tremendous as this act of grace when the Son of the Almighty, that Prince of his Father's royal household, he who had once spoken as Jehovah, he who had conde-scended to come to earth as a babe born in Bethlehem, gave his life in ignominy and pain so that all of the sons and daughters of God, of all generations of time, every one of whom must die, might walk again and live eternally.
>
> This is the wondrous and true story of Christmas. The birth of Jesus in Bethlehem of Judea is preface. The three-year ministry of the Master is prologue. The magnif-icent substance of the story is his sacrifice, the totally self-less act of dying in pain and dishonor and on the cross of Calvary to atone for the sins of all of us.
>
> The epilogue is the miracle of the Resurrection, bring-ing that assurance that "as in Adam all die, even so in Christ shall all be made alive" (1 Cor. 15:22).[3]

Will you remember the journey of the wise men in hope to seek the child and be willing to make the sacrifices necessary to make your own wise man's journey?

The Journey of the Soldiers

The third journey is one we don't usually think about in connection with the Christmas story. It's a dark story, an ugly story, a sad story. This is the journey made by the soldiers of Herod. You remember that God warned the wise men in a dream not to go back to Herod's court and tell him where they had found Jesus, so they went back home by another road, and an angel appeared in a dream to Joseph and told him to take Mary and the baby and flee to Egypt.

But there was no angel who came to the other homes in Bethlehem, warning the mothers and fathers that their infant and toddler boys were in danger. The scriptures tell us:

> When Herod realized that the visitors from the east had tricked him, he was furious. He gave orders to kill all the boys in Bethlehem and its neighborhood who were two years old and younger—in accordance with what he had learned from the visitors about the time when the star had appeared.
>
> In this way what the prophet Jeremiah had said came true: "A sound is heard . . . the sound of bitter crying and weeping. Rachel weeps for her children. She weeps and will not be comforted, because they are all dead." (Matthew 2:16–18.)

This journey to seek the child was very different. Unlike the shepherds, who came with hope, and unlike the wise men, who came with faith, the soldiers came with swords in their hands and murder on their minds. They were seeking the child only to slay him. That doesn't necessarily mean they were evil men, but it does mean they were compartmentalized men. They under-stood the rules. They understood the commands they had received. The thoughts and feelings in their hearts did not matter. Perhaps they enjoyed killing the babies of Bethlehem. Perhaps it made some of them sick. But the babies were still dead at the end.

There are many things that slay the Spirit—and will slay the Spirit at any time, not just at Christmastime. Immorality, cruelty, and dishonesty, even in little things, will slay the Spirit as quickly as a sharp sword. Being lazy, being hard-hearted, being self-indulgent will strangle the Spirit—a slower death, perhaps, than a blade, but just as final.

And there are special challenges that come at Christmastime—many pressures that crowd into already busy schedules, complications caused by the weather, by colds and flu that come with the season, by the fatigue and overload of too many delightful programs and parties to go to, by money worries about presents to buy from a tight budget. These pressures can also make us feel like soldiers under orders, marching to a destination we didn't choose with a task we do not relish.

That's not a very happy feeling to associate with Christmas. Remember that scripture: "The letter killeth, but the spirit giveth life." (2 Corinthians 3:6.) To me, in this context, it means that we need to keep the spirit of Christmas alive. We need to choose the spirit of the law rather than the letter of the law. And we need to grow in the Spirit.

It also means that we have to pay attention to the quality of our spiritual lives and to break down the compartments between parts of our lives. It's not enough that we're doing what our parents and our spouses and our bosses and our teachers and our bishops want us to do, wise and loving and helpful though they are. We need to have our own faith, our own light, and our own testimonies. We have to believe that truth and honor and integrity are important for us individually, not just that they are important principles of the gospel. We have to believe that kindness should be *our* way of life, not just a nice slogan for the Relief Society. We have to speak up in defense of the truth, not just comfort ourselves with the knowledge that we have the truth.

Marian Wright Edelman, a wonderful, warm black woman and the founder and president of the Children's Defense Fund, is someone I really respect. She and her husband, Peter Edelman, who is Jewish, have three grown sons, whom they have raised in both the Christian and the Jewish traditions. She wrote a book entitled *The Measure of Our Success: A Letter to My Children and Yours* about advocacy for children. She graduated from Spelman College, which is a black women's college, and Yale Law school, and has won the MacArthur Prize Fellowship and the Albert Schweitzer Humanitarian Award. A few Christmases ago, she wrote a thoughtful Christmas prayer from the center of her heart as a children's advocate. She said:

> All during the Christmas season, as millions celebrate
> a poor, homeless child Christians call the Savior, I think
> about the . . . millions [of] children becoming destitute,
> homeless, and hungry. . . . Herod is riding across our land
> again.

Then she quoted this prayer, which has appeared in a Christian periodical:

Lord, it is Christmas and
Herod is searching for and destroying our children,
pillaging their houses, corrupting their minds,
killing and imprisoning the sons, orphaning the daughters,
widowing the mothers.

Herod's soldiers are everywhere,
     in government, on Wall Street, in the church
     house, schoolhouse, and moviehouse.

Lead us and our children to safety.

God, we confess that ours is still a world in which
     Herod seems to rule:
the powerful are revered,
the visions of the wise are ignored,
the poor are afflicted,
and the innocent are killed.

You show us that salvation comes
in the vulnerability of a child,
yet we hunger for the "security" of weapons and walls.

You teach us that freedom comes in loving service,
yet we trample on others in our efforts to be "free."

Forgive us, God, when we look to the palace
instead of the stable,
when we heed politicians more than prophets.

Renew us with the spirit of Bethlehem,
that we may be better prepared for your coming.[4]

If you feel like a soldier instead of a shepherd, you can remember that we worship at the stable, not at the palace. If you feel that Christmas has you marching in lockstep toward a destination you don't like very much, step out of line. It is more important to be kind than to be on time. It is more important to show love than to show efficiency. Mother Teresa said, "Kind words can be short and easy to speak, but their echoes are truly endless."[5] Do you have a few seconds to say "Thank you" with a smile, to listen, to push a grocery cart for an elderly woman, to make a phone call or pay a visit that you've been meaning to for a long time? Don't underestimate something as simple as a smile. As one person said, "I've learned that a warm smile beams, 'Welcome to this moment.'"[6] And someone else noted, "Every moment is a gift from God. That's why it's called the *present*."

From the time our boys were very little, Ed and I used to choose a family to provide a Christmas for. Ed was in social work, so he knew families who were in trouble or need. Two particular Christmases stick in my mind, both when our sons were about seven to nine. We learned about the single mother of three children in an apartment building, alone for Christmas. We had to climb many stairs to the top floor, I remember, carrying food for a Christmas dinner and presents that the boys had helped us buy.

I was particularly touched because Ken and Bob had said that, in addition to the presents they bought for the children, they wanted to give the two little boys one of their own presents. Each one took a gaily wrapped package from under our Christmas tree that had his name on it, without even knowing what was in it, and I took a doll to the little girl. With great anticipation Bob and Ken watched as the boys opened the presents—and they were unselfishly delighted to see that one package contained a car and another contained a truck. And they left that car and truck there without a regretful sigh when we left after our visit, happy that the boys were happy with them.

In the second experience, we visited a blind man who lived in a small home. It was late afternoon when we arrived with fruit and cookies, items for a dinner for him, and a small cut tree. There were no lights on when we arrived. Naturally, he didn't need them, but he turned them on for us. He touched the tree and breathed in its fragrance. We'd brought ornaments, too, some that the children had made and some that we'd purchased that had patterns on them so he could feel them. We sang Christmas carols together—"Away in a Manger" and "Silent Night." I will always remember how Bob would carefully select an ornament and hand it to Ken. Ken would take the man's hand, put the ornament in his hand, and then guide his hand to the tree so he could be part of decorating it. There was such joy on the boys' faces, such happiness on the man's.

The boys had made their own Christmas card for him, carefully printing their Christmas greetings on it. We had taken them shopping, and they had each spent a lot of time picking out presents that they thought would be just right. Ken gave him a tie. Bob gave him some gloves. That little home had been silent and dark before we came. When we left, it was sparkling with Christmas lights, but I don't think they were any brighter than the lights of the Christmas spirit that was in our sons' eyes.

Theirs was the errand of angels on those days, not the errands of soldiers.

The Other Journeys

We've talked about three journeys, but actually there are many more. There is the journey that Mary took to Elisabeth as soon as the baby was conceived, and perhaps there's a message there about the kind of loving support we should have to accompany us in our search for the child.

There is also the journey of Joseph, Mary, and Jesus by night and in haste toward Egypt, a reminder that we live in a world where injustice is real and where the innocent must be protected from those who would destroy them. And I hope that we will commit ourselves to speak the truth and speak in defense of those who need the truth as a protection.

And, perhaps most important, there is the journey that Joseph and Mary took toward Bethlehem, when Mary bore the child within herself as a hope and a promise but not yet as a living child. Perhaps that journey can remind us that each journey toward the Savior is a journey of faith and hope and that we cannot hope to find a Savior in the world out there—out in the world around us—unless he is first and foremost within our hearts.

But I want to talk about the journey that we as adults all need to make, and perhaps never more so than at this time of year, and that is the search for the child within us, the little child we should seek to become as we receive the kingdom of heaven and its righteousness. There is a child of faith, and trust, and wonder within us that sometimes cannot be born because of our weariness and our cynicism and because of earlier betrayals.

I suspect that few have escaped some of life's great betrayals: the shattering of love when you give it to someone who will not or cannot return it, or the sharing of love with someone who proves unworthy of it. Some are survivors of childhood sexual abuse or rape or crimes of personal violence, sometimes committed against them by members of their own family. There are those who are surviving the ongoing pain of divorce, of wasted potential, of faltering faith, of bearing the wounds of a beloved child or sibling who has used his or her free agency to make terrible choices that have brought great suffering to himself or herself and others. In your family, or in the family of someone close to you, is someone working through the difficult realizations of homosexuality, of chronic physical illness, of mental or emotional instability, of chemical dependency, of injustice done to you or a loved one, of sorrow, of loneliness, of discouragement?

In each of these circumstances, your hopes for happiness may seem to be betrayed. Pray for the rebirth of that child within you—not that you may be childish but that you may trust in the love and redemptive power of Jesus, who became a little child that he might experience mortality with us and for us and on our behalf.

If you knew my husband, Ed, you would know exactly what I mean by keeping a childlike spirit. He died twelve years ago, and I miss him at Christmas even more keenly than at other times of the year.

Ed loved Christmas so much. He would write to every

missionary in the ward and send them a check. Even before Thanksgiving, he would check out the Christmas-tree lots and start inspecting trees. His mind was always full of others. He always enjoyed thinking of what to give the neighbors, talking over ideas with me and going to shop for presents. He could bestow a bag of apples with such pleasure in the giving that they twinkled like Christmas balls. He loved decorating the trees. Stringing the lights around the doorway and the eaves of the house filled him with delight. In the stores when we were shopping, people used to turn and look at him, because he always had such an irrepressible smile on his face, as if he had just thought of the happiest idea in the world.

He loved Christmas music. If he wasn't singing along with the radio or the stereo, then he was singing along without them, and he hummed along with the carols in elevators and even the Muzak versions in grocery stores and department stores. He always had a contribution and a smile for the Salvation Army bell-ringers. He always had a smile and a kind word for the children who got tired of shopping before their parents were ready to leave the stores. He remembered people who were likely to be alone near the holidays and simply rejoiced in visiting them to give them Christmas wishes.

We have a benjaminus ficus tree about five or six feet tall in our entryway, and it was Ed's idea to decorate it for Christmas one year with little twinkling lights and small bright ornaments. He loved that ficus so much that after Christmas was over, we decorated it with origami cranes for New Year's. And then we decorated it with hearts for Valentine's Day. And then came flowers and bunnies and chicks for Easter. And then flowers for summer, and flags for the Fourth of July. Then came autumn leaves for September, and tiny black cats and jack-o-lanterns for Halloween, and turkeys and cornucopias for Thanksgiving.

I think it was typical of Ed that he found a way for a Christmas idea to spill over into the entire year, so that the first thing we saw as we walked into our home was a decorated tree that brought us a spirit of celebration and thankfulness for our blessings.

Ed had decorated the tree for Easter a little early the year he died. It was several weeks later, almost summer, before I had the heart to take them down, and I shed a few tears as I put the decorations away. I have to confess that I haven't been able to decorate the ficus in our entryway since Ed's death. I haven't had a Christmas tree since he died, and I've been very grateful for assignments that have taken me out of town and for good friends who have shared their trees and the magic of Christmas with me instead, for being able to join Bob and Chris and Ken and Kelle their children for Christmas or to find other worthy projects. But Ed was someone who kept the child alive in himself, and by so doing, he honored the child who was born in Bethlehem.

Conclusion

Think how we began: with President Hunter and his excellent advice about keeping the shower curtain inside the tub. I hope in the thoughts I've shared that you've also had some concepts and insights come to you about the tender and powerful idea of seeking the child this year at Christmas. We looked at the journey of the shepherds, and how they made that journey with faith, taking with them the implements and baggage of their daily life, and then returned to that life refreshed and invigorated. Remember me as a Buddhist child in Hawaii, celebrating Christmas as a secular holiday, loving the togetherness of my family and the color and the pageantry of Christmas, but not yet having my daily life transformed by the living, breathing, reality of a testimony of the Savior.

The second journey to seek the child was the journey of hope of the wise men. They came from afar and traveled for many days. They risked danger, had to go among strangers, and had to leave behind their own people, their own languages, and their own country. Remember Ken and the mashed potatoes, then remember the strangers among you who are perhaps lonely for their own psychological and emotional countries—or even their literal countries—but who have enough hope to continue their search for the child on the basis of starlight.

And the third journey to seek the child was that of the soldiers, who came with swords in their hands, seeking to slay the child. To them, the murder of innocent children was a job. They could not ask whether they were doing good or evil. They could only ask if they were obeying their orders.

There may be times this Christmas season when we feel that we have received marching orders—from our schedules, from our long to-do lists, from our own sense of duty and responsibility. Can we instead seek the spirit of the child in Bethlehem with hands that are swift to serve and feet that make haste to carry us to a place where our love and sympathy are needed? Remember

Ed and his love of Christmas. Seek that spirit of happiness and joy and let it fill you to the brim this Christmas.

There's a beautiful poem by J. Harold Gwynne that encourages us all:

> *It is not far to Bethlehem,*
> *Where lies the newborn King!*
> *It is not far to Bethlehem,*
> *Where holy angels sing.*
>
> *As Wise Men saw the guiding star*
> *That led them where He lay,*
> *The shepherds heard the heavenly song*
> *That first glad Christmas day.*
>
> *We too may go to Bethlehem*
> *And find the Savior Child;*
> *We too may hear the angels sing*
> *Their hymns of mercy mild.*
>
> *Our hearts are God's new Bethlehem*
> *When Christ is born anew.*
> *It is not far to Bethlehem*
> *When he is born in you!*[2]

May the Spirit of Christ be reborn in each of us this Christmas season, and may it be a season of worship, of kindness, of joy, and of rejoicing.

NOTES

1. "Exceeding Great and Precious Promises," *Ensign*, November 1994, 8.
2. Eleanor Knowles, *Howard W. Hunter* (Salt Lake City: Deseret Book, 1994), 281–82.

3. As quoted in "First Presidency Extols Meaning of Christmas," *Ensign,* February 1995, 78.

4. Marian Wright Edelman, *Guide My Feet: Prayers and Meditations on Loving and Working for Children* (Boston: Beacon Press, 1995), 94–95.

5. As quoted in Editors of Conari Press, *Random Acts of Kindness* (Berkeley, Calif.: Conari Press, 1993), 89.

6. Age 50, H. Jackson Brown, Jr., comp., *Live and Learn and Pass It On, Vol. II* (Nashville, Tenn.: Rutledge Hill Press, 1955), 66.

7. J. Harold Gwynne, "It Is Not Far to Bethlehem," in *One Hundred Songs of the Seasons,* compiled by John M. Rasley (Grand Rapids, Mich.: Zondervan, 1977), 62–63.

3

CHRISTMAS PRESENCE

*A*s an educator, *I was always delighted when children* would discover some of the wonderful games that can be played with language in the creation of puns, images, and literalisms—such as, "Have you ever seen a butterfly?" "No, but I've seen the lettuce leaf." Or how about the games you can play with homonyms, such as *horse* and *hoarse?* I would like to share some thoughts about another pair of homonyms: Christmas *presents* and Christmas *presence.*

We all know about the first kind. Christmas presents come wrapped in bright paper with big red bows on them, and we find them under the Christmas tree. The second kind is the awareness that someone else is with us—the Christmas presence of our Savior. The scriptures describe both kinds for us. The first is the present as a gift, and the scriptures refer to us laying our gifts on the altar, kings giving gifts to prophets and other kings, God accepting Abel's gift, and the wise men presenting to the Christ child their gifts of gold and frankincense and myrrh. In the second case, we find Adam and Eve hiding themselves from the presence of God, Moses coming into the presence of Pharaoh, and the commandment in Psalms to come into the presence of the Lord with singing. It is this second kind I want to examine—the presence of the Lord, the presence of his love, the presence of his grace.

As the epistle to the Hebrews tells us, Jesus said, "I will never leave thee, nor forsake thee. So that we may boldly say, The Lord is my helper, and I will not fear what [anyone] shall do unto me. . . . Jesus Christ the same yesterday, and to day, and for ever." (Hebrews 13:5–6, 8.)

Love is the magic that combines both presents and presence in Pearl S. Buck's lovely story about Rob, a fifteen-year-old boy growing up on a farm. His father had always awakened him at four o'clock so he could help milk the cows. Then, a few days before Christmas, he overheard his father tell his mother that he wished he didn't need Rob's help. The boy was always so deeply asleep in the mornings that the father could tell he was famished for his rest.

Hearing his father say those words, Rob suddenly realized that his father loved him. They hadn't talked much about love in their family. The farm took so much time and effort they didn't seem to have need of such things. So for Rob, that discovery of his father's love was a miracle of new awareness, and he wished he had been able to save more money to buy a better present for his father than the necktie he'd purchased at the ten-cent store.

On Christmas Eve that year, as he lay in bed in his attic room, looking out of the window, the stars seemed "bright, much brighter than he ever remembered seeing them, and one star in particular was so bright that he wondered if it were really the Star of Bethlehem." And then it came to him. A stable was just a barn, like their barn. But it was good enough for Mary, Joseph, Jesus, the shepherds, and the wise men. Then he got his wonderful idea—a gift that he could take to a barn for the man he loved most in the world and who loved him:

> He could get up early, earlier than four o'clock, and he could creep into the barn and get all the milking done. He'd do it alone, milk and clean up, and then when his father went in to start the milking, he'd see it all done. And he would know who had done it.
>
> He laughed to himself as he gazed at the stars. It was what he would do, and he mustn't sleep too sound.

He woke himself up time after time, afraid to do more than doze lest he oversleep. Finally, at a quarter to three, he got up, dressed quietly, and sneaked downstairs, avoiding the steps that creaked. Outside, the big star hanging over the barn roof was red-gold.

> He had never milked all alone before, but it seemed almost easy. He kept thinking about his father's surprise. His father would come in and call him, saying that he would get things started while Rob was getting dressed.

He'd go to the barn, open the door, and then he'd go to get the two big empty milk cans. But they wouldn't be waiting or empty; they'd be standing in the milk house, filled.

"What the—" he could hear his father exclaiming.

He smiled and milked steadily, two strong streams rushing into the pail, frothing and fragrant. . . . Milking for once was not a chore. It was something else, a gift to his father who loved him.

When he finished, he poured the milk into the cans and covered them, washed the pail, put everything away, closed the milk house, barred the barn door, and vanished up the stairs like a ghost. He could hear his father getting up as he pulled off his clothes and slipped back into bed. Then his door opened.

"Rob!" his father called. "We have to get up, Son, even if it is Christmas."

"Aw-right," he said sleepily.

"I'll go on out," his father said. "I'll get things started."

The door closed and he lay still, laughing to himself. In just a few minutes his father would know. His dancing heart was ready to jump from his body.

The minutes were endless—ten, fifteen, he did not know how many—and he heard his father's footsteps again. The door opened and he lay still.

"Rob!"

"Yes, Dad—"

"You . . ." His father was laughing, a queer, sobbing sort of a laugh. "Thought you'd fool me, did you?" His father was standing beside his bed, feeling for him, pulling away the cover.

"It's for Christmas, Dad!"

He found his father and clutched him in a great hug. He felt his father's arms go around him. It was dark and they could not see each other's faces.

"Son, I thank you. Nobody ever did a nicer thing—"

"Oh, Dad, I want you to know—I do want to be good!" the words broke from him of their own will. He did not know what to say. His heart was bursting with love.

"Well, I reckon I can go back to bed and sleep," his father said after a moment. "No, hark—the little ones are waked up. Come to think of it, Son, I've never seen you children when you first saw the Christmas tree. I was always in the barn. Come on!"

[Rob] got up and pulled on his clothes again and they went down to the Christmas tree. . . . Oh, what a Christmas, and how his heart had nearly burst again with shyness and pride as his father told his mother and made the younger children listen about how he, Rob, had got up all by himself.

"The best Christmas gift I ever had," [his father repeated,] "and I'll remember it, Son, every year on Christmas morning, so long as I live."[1]

For me, this story captures the essential elements of the homonyms *presence* and *presents*.

Certainly, Rob gave his busy, tired father a gift by doing the milking for him, but he gave his father a much more valued gift by communicating in an unmistakable way that he loved him.

That is the second kind of presence, the gift of being fully present to another person—not distracted or simply dutiful but deeply and timelessly loving.

We all know how busy December can be. There are all the usual chores and carpooling and supervising homework and getting the laundry back into the drawers. There are parties, increased appeals from charities, teenagers who need to be driven to special service projects, food drives in the schools, and Salvation Army bell-ringers standing outside the stores. There are Christmas decorations to be put up and traditional recipes to make and a desire to make things memorable and lovely for families and friends who are under exactly the same pressures that you are. Even for people who live alone, there are more gatherings than usual, Christmas cards to send out, preparations to make, and special celebrations to attend.

No wonder we're tired! No wonder we sometimes feel burdened and exhausted. I'm not saying that you should simplify Christmas or that you should prioritize your activities or that you should put the needy in the community first. You can't pick up a magazine that doesn't already bombard you with good advice. Instead, I want to emphasize the feeling that was in Rob's heart, the feeling that is in my own heart, the special Christmas feeling that you recognize in your own heart. The best present you can give anyone is your own presence, your willingness to be fully present for a neighbor, a child, a spouse, or the individuals in a class you're teaching. I'm talking about making each encounter a loving encounter to which you bring a gracious and loving presence rather than a very long checklist.

It is not my purpose to add to your burdens. I would like instead to lift them if I can. I'm asking you to remember feelings that you've already had and already recognize, the feelings of love remembered that sprang up in your heart as you responded to the story of Rob. I'm asking you to remember the presence of the Savior in your life and in your heart and to let your consciousness of the Savior and his life linger in the front of your mind, that he may be the light by which you carry out your daily tasks and the salt that seasons every taste.

Mother Teresa prays, "Jesus, I believe in Your tender love for me. I love You." Then she reminds us:

> Open your hearts to the love of God which He will give you—He loves you with tenderness. And He will give you [that love], not to keep but to share. . . . We read in the Scripture that God loved the world so much that He gave His Son Jesus who became small, helpless in the womb of His Mother. He was like us in all things except sin. And on coming to His Mother—His Mother, having the presence of Jesus Himself in her womb—she went in haste to serve [Elizabeth]. The fruit of the coming of Jesus is always the need to give Him to others. And she went to serve her cousin who was also with child.
>
> [Mother Teresa continues:] And something very beautiful, something very wonderful happened at their meeting. The first one, first human being to recognize the presence of the coming of Jesus, the son of God . . . the little one in the womb of his mother, leaped with joy. He recognized that [the Savior] had come. And it's so

beautiful to think that God gave that little unborn child the greatness of proclaiming the presence of God, the presence of Jesus on earth.[2]

That's what I'm asking you to do—to "open your heart to God," and to carry the love of Jesus within you as a pregnant woman carries her unborn child within her—to be aware of the Savior's love within you as you would always be aware of that little growing body. Even if you've never experienced pregnancy yourself, you almost certainly have someone close to you who has been pregnant. And maybe you've noticed that it's not always fun? Well, I promise you that there may be times when the awareness of the Christ spirit within will make you a little uncomfortable too. You will sometimes feel a little kick or a jab from it. You will definitely feel yourself stretching from it. But there is also a joy and a gladness that come with that bright love.

I'm recommending that you carry the awareness of Christ within you for a very practical purpose. Once you take your thoughts off Jesus and focus them on yourself, some of the light goes out of your life. Almost as soon as you start thinking about yourself, you begin to have negative thoughts about your problems and inadequacies—you experience feelings of guilt. But you don't need to compare yourself to anyone else. You are okay, just the way you are. Each of us is, with our own needs, our own abilities, our own desires for righteousness, and our own set of obstacles to overcome. Let me remind you of my favorite proverb from the ancient book of Okazaki, chapter 1, verse 1. It's very short, so I encourage you to memorize it. This is how it goes: "Lighten up!" I authorize you to quote this proverb on appropriate occasions—certainly to your family and friends, if the situa-tion warrants, but very frequently to yourself!

Remember, if you're doing the best you can, that's good enough. Don't keep lists of how you've failed or of things you've left undone. Pay attention to what you *have* done. And keep your feelings about the presence of the Christ-spirit within you alive and bright. Sing along, even with those Muzak Christmas carols in the grocery stores. Laugh a lot. Praise your children. Thank them. Do the same to adults. If you only do half of what you wanted to do, or if you do it only half as well as you'd like, pat yourself on half your back. But lighten up! This is the darkest time of the year in the northern hemisphere, but lighten up! The Light of the World is coming once again to us in this season!

With the presence of the Savior in our lives and our hearts, we're prepared to give the gift of our own presence to others. In fact, there won't be any way to avoid doing it. You'll be amazed at how easy it will be, how joyous, how fun! You see, what Rob didn't realize was happening while he was preparing his gift for his father was that he himself was changing. He was becoming a person who was conscious of love in his life and conscious that he had within himself the enormous, miraculous, sacred power to give love to another. Notice what he says to his father at the point where he thought his heart would burst for joy:—"Oh, Dad, I want you to know—I do want to be good!" He didn't think of it in religious terms, at least not as Pearl Buck tells the story; but that's where the power and the impulse truly come from.

How shall we go about giving the gift of our own presence?

Let's think about this whole process in terms of a job description. Usually we get up in the morning and define our lives by tasks. We think, "Let's see. It's Tuesday. I've got to drive the children to school, run to the store for some onions and potatoes, and then go to a business appointment." We focus on the task and think about accomplishing it in the most efficient way possible so that we can get on to the next task. Our job description for the day is to get through the tasks on our checklist.

Now, lists are important. I have long lists myself. But I want you to think about it in a different way. Let's try thinking of the job list as an itinerary. It's a map that takes us where we need to go. But our real job is to be fully present to whomever we are with while we are doing the task. Try to visualize the way Jesus spent his days. Did he get up in the morning and think, "Well, these apostles are still asleep. I've got to roust them out, and we've got to hike over to Bethany today, and I'd better think of two good parables while I'm doing it"? I don't think so. Going to Bethany may have been his itinerary for the day, but he was fully present on the way to his apostles, with the parable of the sower perhaps springing up spontaneously to his lips to tell them first, before it was ready to tell the multitude.

And what about you? Do you have to drive your teenagers to seminary or to school? What a gift! For ten minutes you'll all be in the car together. It's a chance to tell a joke, to remember a family experience, to talk about a worry, to sing a song together, to say thank you, to share appreciation. Your checklist is an itinerary that gets you out to the car and gets the car to where you're going, but your real job is being with the people in that car, your own dear children.

And then perhaps you have to go to the store. Then your job is to be a pleasant presence on the street with the other drivers, to greet the clerk at the store with a smile, and to thank the person at the check-out stand sincerely. You can minister to these people while you are carrying out a task of administration. And the same thing at the business appointment. There's an agenda of items, there is information to be processed, and there are decisions to be made, but the people in the room with you are your task. You can be fully present with them and communicate your regard for them by letting the love of the Savior in your heart speak through your words and shine through your eyes. Happiness is contagious. It communicates confidence, respect, regard.

Let me cite some examples. Joseph W. Charles is a cheerful black man who waved hello to commuters during rush hour for thirty years from his front yard beside one of the heavily traveled streets in Berkeley, California. He started waving in October 1962 and "retired," at the age of eighty-two, in October 1992. People loved it. A woman who is a municipal judge said, "I used to go out of my way just to wave at him. When you saw him it made your whole day." The mayor said, "He's lifted the community's spirits every morning for thirty years."[3] Think what a gift of *presence* Joseph Charles gave to his community.

You will recall in Charles Dickens's great story *A Christmas Carol* the scene where the ghost of Jacob Marley comes back to visit his old partner, Ebenezer Scrooge, to warn him to mend his ways. Scrooge observes hesitantly, "You were always a good man of business, Jacob!"

But the shackled ghost does not appreciate the compliment. He wails, "Mankind was my business! The common good was my business! The wretched beggarwoman with her child was my business! I walked among humanity with my eyes cast down." He warns Ebenezer that Scrooge's own eyes are fastened too much on business, as Jacob Marley's had been, and informs him that if he will lift his eyes to the faces of those around him, he will see shining in their eyes the blessed star of Bethlehem. When Scrooge has been transformed by the visits of the ghosts of Christmas Past, Present, and Future, he is then able to give the gift of his presence—a happy, loving presence that listens with appreciation to the Christmas carols, that observes Tiny Tim with concern and affection, that greets the gentlemen collecting funds for the poor with courtesy and generosity.

Another person who was something of a genius in being fully present to people was Gandhi. It took a lifetime of effort to root the selfishness out of his own nature, he said; but toward the end of his life, those who were close to Gandhi were amazed how, in those years, he met the demands upon him with endless patience, courage, resilience, and irrepressible good humor.

> Every minute was given over to others, beginning with the steady stream of visitors who came from all over the world for every conceivable reason: to get an interview for the *New York Times*, to settle some question of . . . voting rights, to argue with his opinions on birth control or to get help in disciplining an unruly child. Beyond those

who requested interviews stood the mute crowds who had come just to watch this "poor little man . . ." who had made the smallest detail of his life a joy to watch. With Gandhi, who was at home with himself wherever he went, they immediately felt at home: as if they had always belonged at Sevagram, and Gandhi's huge adopted family were their own. Gandhi gave them all the same attention, fitting each person somewhere into his own close sched-ule for the day, talking to them on his morning walk, or at breakfast, or over the spinning wheel. . . . [He said], "You may not waste a grain of rice or a scrap of paper, . . . and similarly a minute of your time. It is not ours. . . . We are trustees for the use of it."[4]

He did not consider that he was wasting time when he was talking to people. On the contrary, he considered that to be his most important task. He gave the gift of his presence always, and through his influence people discovered new power in them-selves to deal lovingly and patiently with others.

And what about giving the gift of our presence in our church callings? For several years now, the General Authorities have emphasized that our job is to minister to those we serve, not simply to administer a program. The programs are important. They give structure to our group life. But more important, they provide the opportunities to be together so that we can truly minister to each other.

One of the missionaries who served with us when my hus-band, Ed, was called to be a mission president in Japan, lives in the Salt Lake Valley. He told me that his stake leaders recently decided to institute a new policy in connection with their home teaching program. All of the assigned brethren were supposed to have their home teaching completed by the second week of the month and report it. During the third week of the month, the quorum leaders were supposed to finish up the visits that hadn't been made and then report to the stake leaders. And during the fourth week of the month, the stake presidency said that *they* would finish up what hadn't been completed.

"Oh," I asked my missionary, "and how did it go?"

He laughed a little. "I was out of town during the first week of the month, so I got several calls urging me to go and reminding me to report. It was probably okay. But basically all of the calls were making me feel guilty about not going. I felt pressured, and it seemed to me like the statistics were being emphasized instead of the people I visit. I resented this new policy for making me feel guilty."

"Oh," I said, "and how did it work?"

He smiled a little sadly. "I don't think it worked very well," he said. "I'm assigned to visit two widows, a single sister, an inactive family, and a young inactive man dying of cancer. My supervisor had always been very concerned about them as individuals. But this month, in all of the calls I got—and there were probably half a dozen—no one asked me, not even once, how any of the people I visit were doing. Everyone seemed to be so worried about the numbers that they didn't have time for the people."

To me, this is a very clear example of the difference between administering a program and ministering to the people we serve. Sometimes we get caught up in counting the sheep instead of feeding them. Sometimes we're more worried about empty chairs than we are about empty hearts. Our church callings can provide wonderful opportunities to minister to people if we have our hearts centered on the light that Jesus brings. In this example, my missionary felt as though he was being treated like a worker who needed to be nagged to fulfill a contract rather than as a colleague who shared a covenant. We are people of the covenant, but sometimes we behave as though we were people of a contract. And there is a difference between a contract and a covenant.

A contract spells out objectives, compensation, working conditions, benefits, incentive opportunities, constraints, and timetables while specifying schedules and penalties for noncompliance. Is that how we feel about our church assignments? We're called to do a certain job; and when we accept it, we make a sort of contract with the bishop to show up at a certain time in a certain place, with the manual or some other tool in our hand, and to perform to a certain level.

We're all covenant makers in the Church; but to get a different perspective on it, listen to what businessman Max De Pree has to say about covenantal relationships:

> The majority of us who work can properly be classified as volunteers. [And that's *definitely* all of us in the Church. We're *all* volunteers.] The best people working for organizations are *like* volunteers. Since they could probably find good jobs with any number of groups, they choose to work somewhere for reasons less tangible than

salary or position. Volunteers do not need contracts; they
need covenants.

Covenantal relationships enable corporations and
institutions to be hospitable to the unusual person and to
unusual ideas. Covenantal relationships enable participa-
tion to be practiced and inclusive groups to be formed. . . .
Covenantal relationships tolerate risk and forgive errors.
. . . Covenantal relationships . . . induce freedom, not paral-
ysis. A covenantal relationship rests on shared commitment to ideas, to issues, to values, to goals, and to man-
agement processes . . . [to] love, warmth, [and] personal
chemistry. . . . Covenantal relationships are open to influence. They fill deep needs, and they enable work to have
meaning and to be fulfilling. Covenantal relationships
reflect unity and grace and poise. They are an expression
of the sacred nature of relationships.[5]

Max De Pree is talking about creating a covenantal relationship in the workplace. How much more, then, should we, the
people of covenant, create covenantal relationships in our asso-
ciations at church? Where should we better cherish diversity,
really listen to people, and give fully the gift of our presence than
at church? If your Relief Society has a quilting project, you have
the wonderful and delightful task of associating with the other
sisters around that quilting frame in joyous sisterhood, in
respectful listening, and in honest sharing. Oh yes, you inciden-
tally have the opportunity of finishing a quilt. But your real job is
the women next to you. They are your neighbors, your sisters in

covenant, the persons you are to minister to for that hour you are together.

When you go visiting teaching, your commitment isn't simply to show up with a photocopy of the message from the *Ensign* in your hand. When you go home teaching, it's not to merely satisfy some report. It's to show up with the love of Jesus in your heart and to minister to that person's needs with care and respect—with the gift of your full presence. And, while you're ministering, don't forget your companion and his or her needs as you have the opportunity to be together for that time.

We cannot fully give the gift of our presence if we're worried about the worthiness of the recipient, so let's seize with gratitude the scriptural commandment not to judge. There are those in the Church whose assignment and calling it is to judge, but if that is not your assigned duty or responsibility, then follow the Savior's admonition to "judge not, that ye be not judged." (Matthew 7:1.) By so commanding us, he has lifted a great burden from us. We don't need to judge the need of someone who holds a sign that reads "Hungry and Homeless." We don't need to judge the motives of someone at church who gossips about a friend. We don't need to judge the righteousness of another individual. We can just concentrate on loving them and being fully with them. We don't need to solve their problem or to fix them so they don't have a problem. We don't need to turn our lives over to them. But for the few moments we are together, we can be fully, lovingly together.

We don't need to judge ourselves, either. We don't need to compare our scriptural knowledge to anyone else's or to assess ourselves as inadequate or unworthy. We can simply be free to love and be loved. By doing so, we will find much to love and many ways to show appreciation and caring.

This is my twelfth Christmas without my husband, Ed. He was one of the most appreciative people in the world. I remember, the first winter after we moved to Salt Lake City from Denver, how impressed Ed was when the street department sent their big trucks and snowplows out after the first serious snowstorm and had our streets cleared the same morning. He wondered, "Does anyone tell these people how much we appreciate them?" He thought that probably didn't happen very often, so he visited the neighbors on the streets near us, explained his idea, and asked if they'd like to chip in a couple of dollars.

Then he went to the market, where he bought a crate of apples, a crate of oranges, some doughnuts, and some other goodies before driving to the street department's supervisor's office—I'm not even sure where it was or how he found it. But he just drove up, carried in those things, put them down, and explained where we lived. "I don't know if anyone has said thank you for the wonderful service you performed," he said, "but I know that the whole neighborhood appreciated it, and I'm just saying thank you for all of us."

The supervisor was absolutely overwhelmed. "Nobody ever says thank you to us," he exclaimed. "We only hear the complaints if we don't get the streets cleaned off in time to please people."

Now, this wasn't part of Ed's church job, but I think he thought it was part of his job as a Christian. And think of the ripple effect of Ed's kindly gesture! He certainly could have done something else. He could have made a phone call or written a note. He could have driven straight to the store without involving the neighbors. But instead, he made the neighbors aware of the service they had received and gave them a channel through which to say thank you. They thanked him for that opportunity. And imagine how the snowplow operators felt! Our neighbor to the west, who had lived there for many years, told Ed in the spring, "Our streets have never been cleaner!"

So when it comes to church callings, can we be a little less task-oriented and a little more people-oriented? Let us consider our church assignments as opportunities to give the gift of our presence to those to whom our assignment takes us. Remember that we have a covenantal relationship with them, not a contractual relationship with them—just as we do with our families. Give yourself the great pleasure of not judging but just enjoying and of finding many ways of showing appreciation.

I indicated that I hoped to lift some burdens, not add to them. But if I were to stop here, this might be a discouraging message. I've described expectations for warm, caring, loving interactions. Of course everyone wants them—wants to give them and receive them. But the reality is that such interactions may be very time-consuming and sometimes frustrating. Sometimes they are not answered in kind or even understood. So we need to consider the most important presence of all, and that's the presence of the Savior in our lives.

We are all at different levels in our experiences with and our understandings of Christ. Let me tell you a story about the first

Christmas Ed and I spent in Utah. Our first landlady was Sophronia Forsberg, a wonderful, lively woman who had been a state legislator and was an outspoken woman far in advance of her day. She treated Ed and me like members of her own family, and we were invited to join in her family's celebration at Christmastime. We admired the tree, sparkling with ornaments and glittering with lights. We sang Christmas carols, many of which we already knew. (I had been born into a Buddhist family, but Ed had been raised a Congregationalist, so he had a head start on me in Christmas carols.) We read the Christmas story from the scriptures.

And then we gathered around the table for the Christmas feast. Among the many delicious things we ate, one dish seemed to have special importance. It was a rice pudding with a mysterious penny hidden in it. Ed and I were intrigued and bewildered. Obviously, this penny was very important, because we were told that whoever got it would be lucky all year long. We were just as curious as everyone else to see who would get the penny. But I had a question I was a little afraid to ask: What did the rice pudding and the penny have to do with the birth of Jesus? Or was the penny in the pudding significant in the Church in some way that the missionaries hadn't told us about?

We didn't know. But we soon found out that it really didn't have very much to do with either one. Aunt Frone's family was Scandinavian, and when they joined the Church, they brought this custom from their own culture into their Mormon observance of Christmas. It was really a winter's solstice custom or a New Year's custom, thought to bring good luck for the coming year. But there Ed and I were, two Japanese-Hawaiians, observing a Scandinavian custom as part of this new Mormon Christmas in Utah and trying to make sense of it.

Sometimes we get confused about what's gospel and what's tradition. Sometimes we're not sure if what we're experiencing is the spirit of Christ or a traditional part of Mormon culture that seems right because it's familiar, much loved, and part of our family life. We need to keep all of the parts of culture and tradition that are meaningful and that work for us, but let's not confuse them with the core of the gospel. Let's not mistake them for the spirit of our Savior. Ed and I served rice pudding with a lucky penny in it at many Christmas dinners while our boys were growing up, and to us it represented the Christian spirit and loving hospitality of an Aunt Frone, who opened not only her home but also her heart to two Japanese-American converts from Hawaii.

I thought of the rice pudding experience often when touring the stakes of Japan and Korea. I saw the sisters there struggling to understand the Church program, polite but bewildered about some of the instructions in the handbook that still, despite all of the efforts at making them non—culture specific, assume an American setting. I think we could not have succeeded if the spirit of the Savior and the Holy Ghost had not been there to whisper that we are all sisters, that our job is to love the Lord and to love each other. When we have the gift of the presence of Christ and the Holy Ghost, then we can find ways to express that love according to our circumstances and the circumstances of others.

But the presence of Christ comes first. We cannot give the gift of loving regard to another human being unless we feel in our own hearts the loving regard of the Savior and sense how he cherishes us. When we have those feelings, it is almost impossible for us to treat others in unloving ways. Our love for the other person and our happiness at being in that person's presence will spring up and overflow from our hearts spontaneously, as Rob's love did for his father, as Ed's love did for the men on the snow removal crews, as Aunt Frone's love did for Ed and me, and as the Savior's love does for all of us.

We understand from our Sunday School lessons that we need to fast and pray, and read the scriptures and ponder them, to get the Spirit in our lives. Gandhi got up at three or four in the morning to pray and meditate. But for very busy people, especially if you have been up till two with the baby, where does the time come from to seek this kind of renewal? It could be another burden on you, if you think you must squeeze another hour out of the day for scripture study and meditation. And when we think about squeezing, then we've got the wrong job description.

Christ is already with us. The gift of the Holy Ghost—which means the continual presence of the Holy Spirit—has already been conferred upon us. It is as much a matter of *remembering* as it is of *doing* another project. Remember that Christ is the Light of the World, and that his light is the same light which "enlighteneth your eyes, which is the same light that quickeneth your understandings; which light proceedeth forth from the presence of God to fill the immensity of space." (D&C 88:11–12.) Instead of just looking at the objects illuminated by the light, look at the Light itself. Christ is that Light. When we are aware of his presence, then we are aware of his love for everything around us. We simply cannot avoid loving others.

How can we become more aware of the presence of Christ in our lives? I have a few suggestions. Sing as you go about your duties. I love to sing Christmas carols all year long, and I love the month of December because I can sing them without people looking at me in a strange way.

Perhaps you would love to have an hour or two to pray without interruption, but the pace of your life does not allow you that luxury right now. That's all right; keep a prayer in your heart. I pray continually—while I'm driving, while I'm riding in the elevator, while I'm pushing a shopping cart.

Remember: "God so loved *the world,* that he gave his only begotten Son, that whosoever believeth in him should not perish, but have everlasting life." (John 3:16; emphasis added.) The Savior is not offended at the world. He helped his Father and our Father create it. He doesn't resent the world. He came here to dwell in it with us. He understands that we must live in the world and make our living in the world. He doesn't demand that we leave the world before we are worthy to approach him. He is here with us in the world.

Remember his promise: "I will never leave thee, nor forsake thee. So that we may boldly say, The Lord is my helper, and I will not fear what [anyone] shall do unto me." (Hebrews 13:5–6.) He will not leave *us!* He will not forsake *us!* He gives *us* power and faith and gifts. His grace is sufficient for *us!* Every time we partake of the sacrament, he repeats his promise to us:

his Spirit will always be with us—when? When "we always remember him."

This Christmas season and for the rest of our lives, may we remember the difference between *presence* and *presents*. Remember the story of Rob and how love was born in his heart when he realized that his father loved him and how that love found expression in his best Christmas present ever. May we give to our families and friends the gift of our full presence. May we minister to others through our church callings using our full presence, rather than focusing on administering programs. May we abandon the petty indulgence of judging others in favor of the deep joy of loving others. May we find many ways to say thank you, to express appreciation, and to value others.

This Christmas particularly, think about your own understanding of the gospel and about your neighbor's understanding of the gospel. I'm glad Aunt Frone put that penny in the rice pudding and served it for Christmas dessert. It became a bond of sharing between us, all of us far from our ancestral lands. But if we hadn't asked her why the penny was in the pudding and what it meant—even though we were afraid such a question would show our ignorance of some important gospel principle—and if Aunt Frone hadn't been willing to share the answer, it might have become a barrier between us. Will you think about what might be pennies and rice puddings to you, and then think about the stranger in your midst who is watching with big eyes, trying to understand, and who is maybe just a little afraid to ask a question? Will you, for all our sakes, answer that question, share the book so you can sing the Christmas carols together, and maybe see that he or she gets an extra big helping of the rice pudding?

May we be continually conscious of Christ's presence in our lives. May we remember his life and death, his atonement and his grace, his love and his mercy. May we find joy in his presence, and may our awareness of his presence shine forth from our eyes and illuminate our speech. And may we always remember, at this time of presents, the gift the Father gave us by sending to us his beloved Son, that we may rejoice in that gift with thanksgiving and gladness.

NOTES

1. Pearl S. Buck, "Christmas Day in the Morning," in *Prentice Hall Literature: Silver*, 2d ed. [no editor] (Englewood Cliffs, N. J.: Prentice Hall, 1991), 21–24.

2. Dorothy S. Hunt, sel. and ed., *Love: A Fruit Always in Season: Daily Meditations from the Words of Mother Teresa of Calcutta* (San Francisco: Ignatius Press, 1987), 142–44.

3. "Waving Man Waves Good-bye to 30 Years of Waving Hello," *Deseret News*, 7–8 Oct. 1992, World/Nation, A3.

4. Eknath Easwaran, *Gandhi the Man*, 2d ed. (1973; Petaluma, Calif.: Nilgiri Press for Blue Mountain Center of Meditation, distributed by Random House, 1978), 131.

5. Max De Pree, *Leadership Is an Art* (New York: Bantam Doubleday Dell Publishing Group, 1989), 27–28, 60.

4

A Nephite Christmas

I have been in many homes during the Christmas season, and I know how beautifully homes can reflect the Christmas spirit in our hearts. There are beautiful Christmas trees, twinkling with ornaments and sparkling with lights. There are brightly decorated packages with bright bows. There are wreaths of greenery. There are candles. There are the luscious scents of Christmas cookies baking or potpourri scenting the air or the delicious fragrance of wassail mingling with the sharp smell of the Christmas tree. Sometimes a fire is crackling in the fireplace. Christmas carols are wafting through the air from the radio or the stereo.

And in an honored place is a nativity set with a beautiful mother, a stalwart father, a gentle big-eyed cow, a patient donkey, three wise men in exotic costumes, and humble shepherds with awe and reverence on their faces and a lamb in their arms.

And all of them are looking at a baby. Sometimes the beautiful young mother is holding the baby tenderly in her arms and sometimes he is lying in a manger filled with straw, but he is the centerpiece of their attention, the center of the nativity set, and the center of the Christmas spirit in each home.

These nativity sets are of all kinds—from all kinds, from all cultures, in all kinds of materials. Some are very simple—just the Holy Family. Others have figures from the whole village.

Maybe you have gone to Temple Square to see the figures in the nativity presented there. They are life-size and made with a new process so that they look more lifelike. But the point of that large nativity set is the same as the smallest or the most unusual. It's about that baby—and we feel the same awe as the shepherds as we struggle to understand how a newborn baby can be the point toward which all of human history has been moving. Even before the earth was created, its reason for being hinged on the existence of this baby. And even after this earth has passed into another existence, it will be because of this baby.

Yet he was an ordinary baby to all appearances. That beautiful young mother had carried him in her womb for nine months, just as each one of us grew and stretched and was nurtured by our own mothers who gave birth to us in exactly the same way as Mary.

It is important for us to understand how our feelings about Christmas are focused on this baby—this apparently ordinary baby who was really so extraordinary. Think of the Christmas carols in our hymnbook: "Oh, Come, All Ye Faithful." Come where? Come to Bethlehem. Why? Because, like the shepherds and the wise men, that's where we behold the baby. "Angels We Have Heard on High." Where? Singing to the shepherds. Why? Because the Savior has been born. "Silent night! Holy night! / All is calm, all is bright." Where? "Round yon virgin mother and child."

"Once in Royal David's City." Where is royal David's city? Why, it's Bethlehem, the city of David, where Joseph and Mary went to be taxed and where she brought forth her firstborn son. "Away in a Manger." Why a manger? Because that's where Mary put the baby. "It came upon the midnight clear, / That glorious song of old, / From angels bending near the earth / To touch their harps of gold." It's another song about the birth of the Christ child. "O Little Town of Bethlehem"—it's another song about the little village where Christ was born.

Now do you know why I've refreshed your memory about nativity sets and given you a guided tour of the section of the hymnbook devoted to Christmas hymns? It's because I want you to become even more aware of something we already know: that Christmas is about a baby.

This is hardly news. In fact, it's almost impossible to think of Christmas without thinking of that baby and everything centered on him for that first Christmas—tired but happy Mary and Joseph, angel songs, wondering shepherds, and exotic wise men. But that's exactly what I want you to do.

I want you to think about Christmas with no Mary, no Joseph, no angels, no shepherds, no adorable woolly lamb, no stable, no donkey, no cow, no manger, no wise men, no star, no singing hosts in the heavens, and especially no baby.

Christmas without the Christmas Story

But if all of these things are gone, what's left? How can you even say that there's Christmas at all? Well, this is exactly the situation that the Nephites were in. They didn't know any of this story. For them, the Christmas story was not this beautiful tableau of the Holy Family in a stable on a special night made radiant with stars and angel song. It was something that happened far away that they were given only tiny glimpses of by their prophets.

Let's look at three of those prophetic glimpses that constitute the Nephite Christmas story. The first is the vision of Nephi, the son of Lehi. The second is Samuel the Lamanite's prophecies to the Nephites. And the third is the experiences of Nephi and son of Helaman as those prophecies were fulfilled.

First Nephi's Vision of Mary

They knew about Mary and Jesus as a baby because Nephi, the first Nephi, recorded in his vision of the tree with the glorious white fruit, that he saw her holding Jesus in her arms. He says:

> I looked and beheld the great city of Jerusalem. . . . And I beheld the city of Nazareth; and in the city of Nazareth I beheld a virgin, and she was exceedingly fair and white. (1 Nephi 11:13.)

You remember that Nephi was still only a few hours' travel from Jerusalem, and unlike all of the Nephite prophets who came after him, he actually knew what Jerusalem and Nazareth looked like because he'd seen them in person. Then he continues:

> And an angel came down and stood before me; and he said unto me: Nephi, what beholdest thou?
>
> And I said unto him: A virgin, most beautiful and fair above all other virgins.
>
> . . . And he said unto me: Behold, the virgin whom thou seest is the mother of the Son of God, after the manner of the flesh.
>
> . . . And I looked and beheld the virgin again, bearing a child in her arms. (1 Nephi 11:14–15, 18, 20.)

Nephi didn't see stables, or oxen, or donkeys. No shepherds and no lambs. No wise men and no camels. Not even singing angels. The only angel was the one explaining to Nephi what he was seeing.

Nephi had another couple of glimpses of Jesus:

> And I looked and beheld the Redeemer of the world, of whom my father had spoken; and I also beheld the prophet who should prepare the way before him. And the Lamb of God went forth and was baptized of him; and after he was baptized, I beheld the heavens open, and the Holy Ghost come down out of heaven and abide upon him in the form of a dove. (1 Nephi 11:27.)

Nephi saw Jesus choose his twelve apostles, and he saw a few scenes from Jesus' ministry.

I beheld the Lamb of God going forth among the children of men. And I beheld multitudes of people who were sick, and who were afflicted with all manner of diseases, and with devils and unclean spirits. . . . And they were healed by the power of the Lamb of God; and the devils and the unclean spirits were cast out. (1 Nephi 11:31.)

Well, we seem to have moved on from the Christmas story pretty fast, haven't we? No wise men. No camels. No shepherds. And the only lamb is Jesus Christ himself, the Lamb of God.

And then comes this terrible event that can't possibly be part of the joyous, radiant Christmas story:

> And it came to pass that the angel spake unto me again, saying: Look! And I looked and beheld the Lamb of God, that he was taken by the people; yea, the Son of the everlasting God was judged of the world; and I saw and bear record.
>
> And I, Nephi, saw that he was lifted up upon the cross and slain for the sins of the world. (1 Nephi 11:32–33.)

So, if we were Nephites, that would be the Christmas story: a mother holding a baby, a moment of ministry, and then a cruel and agonizing death. What kind of a Christmas story is that? No gold. No myrrh. No frankincense. Blood, and pain, and death.

And that's the Christmas story that the other Book of Mormon prophets repeated and taught the people and prophesied about for the next six hundred years.

Samuel the Lamanite

Now, let's go ahead about five hundred and ninety-five years to Samuel the Lamanite. When this Lamanite prophet came among the wicked Nephites, they didn't want to hear about his Christmas story or any other, for that matter, but he told them anyway. Let's turn to Helaman 14:2. Here's what he told the people:

> Behold, I give unto you a sign; for five years more cometh, and behold, then cometh the Son of God to redeem all those who shall believe on his name.
>
> And behold, this will I give unto you for a sign at the time of his coming; for behold, there shall be great lights in heaven, insomuch that in the night before he cometh there shall be no darkness, insomuch that it shall appear unto man as if it was day.
>
> Therefore, there shall be one day and a night and a day, as if it were one day and there were no night; and this shall be unto you for a sign; for ye shall know of the rising of the sun and also of its setting; therefore they shall know of a surety that there shall be two days and a night; nevertheless the night shall not be darkened; and it shall be the night before he is born.
>
> And behold, there shall a new star arise, such an one as ye never have beheld; and this also shall be a sign unto you.
>
> . . . And it shall come to pass that whosoever shall believe on the Son of God, the same shall have everlasting life. (Helaman 14:2–5, 8.)

Still no baby, no shepherds, no wise men, but the star is a little more like it—stars and wonders in the heaven, even if there is no angelic chorus.

But the beauty and wonder and awesomeness of this amazing sky of light that transcends the sun and conquers the night has another half to it—a dark half. Samuel the Lamanite goes straight on to another prophecy. Let's start with verse 20:

> But behold, [I give] . . . unto you . . . another sign, a sign of his death, behold, in that day that he shall suffer death the sun shall be darkened and refuse to give his light unto you; and also the moon and the stars; and there shall be no light upon the face of this land, even from the time that he shall suffer death, for the space of three days, to the time that he shall rise again from the dead.
>
> Yea, . . . there shall be thunderings and lightnings for the space of many hours, and the earth shall shake and tremble; and the rocks . . . shall be broken up;
>
> Yea, they shall be rent in twain, and shall ever after be found in seams and in cracks, and in broken fragments upon the face of the whole earth. . . .
>
> And behold, there shall be great tempests, and there shall be many mountains laid low, like unto a valley, and there shall be many places which are now called valleys which shall become mountains. . . .
>
> And many highways shall be broken up, and many cities shall become desolate.
>
> And many graves shall be opened, and shall yield up many of their dead; and many saints shall appear unto many. (Helaman 14:20–25.)

Nephi, the Son of Helaman

Then Samuel the Lamanite disappeared from the walls of Zarahemla and from the records of the Nephites. Suppose you had been in Zarahemla. What image would you have of the Christmas story? You might remember a beautiful young woman holding a baby if you were well versed in the ancient scriptures, but I tend to think that it wouldn't have been your most powerful image of the Christmas story. Instead, I think you would have thought first of this amazing prophecy of Samuel the Lamanite: a day, a night, and a day in which there was no darkness.

Did believing poets write Christmas carols about this day, night, and day? Did painters try to paint it? Can you imagine images of Christmas consisting mostly of Mary, baby Jesus, incredible light, and then the signs of Jesus' death? No Joseph. No shepherds. No stable. No wise men. No angels.

This is about where matters stood as time went along until the time of Jesus' birth approached. The Nephites knew nothing of Zacharias being struck dumb in the temple. They knew nothing about Elisabeth conceiving long after she was too old to bear a child. They knew nothing about Elisabeth's young cousin, Mary, in Nazareth. They knew nothing about a betrothal that was almost called off because the bride was pregnant before the wedding. They'd never heard of Caesar Augustus and his tax. They didn't know anything, in other words, about all the ways of preparing for the advent of this baby that were occurring in the Old World. It was just the same old Nephite world: seed-time and harvest and people getting rich and then people getting proud and wars between the Nephites and the Lamanites.

This was the situation at the beginning of the record kept by Nephi the son of Helaman. With the eye of faith he and the believers saw the "greater signs and greater miracles" that were the equivalent of Zacharias and Elisabeth—even though we don't know what they were. But those without the eye of faith taunted the believers with the idea that the time for Samuel's sign had passed and nothing had happened. The sorrow of the believers at the idea was so great that it increased the cruelty of their tormenters, and they issued a proclamation of execution for the believers if the day, the night, and the day of perfect brightness did not occur by a specific date. (See 3 Nephi 1:4–9.)

Are we starting to see a pattern here? The birth of the Savior—what message could be more glorious? And the execution of all believers—which threat could be harsher? Light and darkness come together in this message, just as they did in the message of Nephi the son of Lehi and in the message of Samuel the Lamanite.

This was the situation in which the next part of the Nephite Christmas story occurs:

> Now it came to pass that when Nephi, the son of Nephi, saw this wickedness of his people, his heart was exceedingly sorrowful.
>
> And it came to pass that he went out and bowed himself down upon the earth, and cried mightily to his God in behalf of his people, yea, those who were about to be destroyed because of their faith in the tradition of their fathers.
>
> And it came to pass that he cried mightily unto the

Lord all that day; and behold, the voice of the Lord came unto him, saying:

Lift up your head and be of good cheer; for behold, the time is at hand, and on this night shall the sign be given, and on the morrow come I into the world, to show unto the world that I will fulfil all that which I have caused to be spoken by the mouth of my holy prophets.

. . . And it came to pass that the words which came unto Nephi were fulfilled, according as they had been spoken; for behold, at the going down of the sun there was no darkness.

. . . And it came to pass also that a new star did appear, according to the word. (3 Nephi 1:10–13, 15, 21.)

Well, you know what happened next. This was incontrovertible evidence that Samuel the Lamanite had spoken the truth. He had predicted something that had never happened before in the history of the world, something that nobody could even imagine how it was possible to happen. It made believers out of skeptics, strengthened the faith of those whose faith was wavering, and confirmed with sure knowledge the faith of those who had not doubted.

But the Christmas story wasn't over for the Nephites. In the Old World, the shepherds went back to their sheep. The wise men left their gifts and went back to their far country, prudently taking a detour to avoid Jerusalem. Angels came to warn Joseph to take Mary and the baby and flee to Egypt to save Jesus' life. It wasn't just business as usual in Palestine. John the Baptist was growing up with his fierce mission of salvation and redemption burning on his lips. And Jesus, even though he grew up quietly learning the skills of carpentry, knew that he had an assignment from his Father, who was not Joseph, that had nothing to do with carpentry.

But in Zarahemla, that day and night and day of perfect brightness had passed and was receding further into the past with every day. Unbelief rose among the people and stole them away from the paths of faith. The Gadianton robbers became so strong that they could offer pitched battle to the Nephites. The political and social system was in shambles. Perhaps some read the prophecies of Nephi the son of Lehi and thought about the ministry of healing and teaching that Jesus Christ was conducting on the other side of the world, but it was far away and the prophecies were long ago, and meanwhile their lives were in danger right now, today!

And that was the condition among the Nephites when the Christmas story was finally completed for them—when, after six hundred years of glimpses and predictions of joy accompanied by terrible sorrows and great discontinuities in the story, they finally had the privilege of Christ coming among them to minister unto them in person and to receive their worship.

Throughout the Christmas story, the beautiful parts have been mingled with terrible parts, but this time, the terrible part came first. Earthquakes ripped the rocks apart. The sea heaved itself from its bed. Mountains fell. Valleys rose. Cities disappeared. The people perished. A stupefying, hideous darkness clamped down over the land, smothering any fire. And the first voice they heard was not a voice of comfort or consolation. No angel chorus sang of peace and goodwill. Instead, they heard this terrifying message:

> Wo, wo, wo unto this people; wo unto the inhabitants of the whole earth except they shall repent; for the devil laugheth, and his angels rejoice, because of the slain of the fair sons and daughters of my people; and it is because of their iniquity and abominations that they are fallen!
>
> Behold, that great city Zarahemla have I burned with fire, and the inhabitants thereof. (3 Nephi 9:2–3.)

And the catalog of carnage continued—city after city, land after land, with people after people wiped out, erased, destroyed.

And then came the message of consolation and promise, the good tidings of great joy:

> O all ye that are spared because ye were more righteous than they, will ye not now return unto me, and repent of your sins, and be converted, that I may heal you?
>
> Yea, verily I say unto you, if ye will come unto me ye shall have eternal life. Behold, mine arm of mercy is extended towards you, and whosoever will come, him will I receive; and blessed are those who come unto me.
>
> Behold, I am Jesus Christ the Son of God. I created the heavens and the earth, and all things that in them are. I was with the Father from the beginning. I am in the Father, and the Father in me; and in me hath the Father glorified his name. (3 Nephi 9:13–15.)

You know the rest of the Nephite Christmas story too. It wasn't just a few shepherds and wise men who came to a lowly stable. It was an entire people—all of the survivors of the Nephites—who gathered at their temple in Bountiful to touch the Savior, each one; kneel before him; bathe his pierced feet with their tears; see angels minister to their little children; hear the Savior pray to the Father on their behalf; and accept the sacrament in token of his sacrifice for them. Their Christmas story was not with a baby but with the resurrected and glorified Lord.

Perhaps you were thinking that there's not much of a Christmas story without the lamb and the stable and the star and the manger. But maybe if we'd been in that congregation at the temple in Bountiful, experiencing the fullness of joy in the Nephite Christmas story, we would wonder why a manger and a donkey were all that important in the first place.

Uniting the Two Kinds of Christmas Story

Let's look again at where we have come. We began with the dear old beloved and familiar story of a baby in Mary's loving arms with Joseph protective and watchful as the humble shepherds heard the angel song and came to the stable bringing a woolly lamb, with the wise men following a new star to find Jesus too. This is our Christmas story, and because we have grown up hearing it and seeing it and singing it since before we can remember, we can forget that it has two parts. Along with its wonder and peace and glory comes the fact that no woman gives birth without pain and blood. No baby is born without distress and struggle. Sometimes we also forget that the shepherds and the wise men were followed by the soldiers of Herod with swords in their hands to kill every baby boy in Bethlehem under the age of two.

And then we looked at the Christmas story that the Nephites would have known: the glimpse of Mary holding her newborn child, followed by a glimpse of Jesus in the waters of baptism, Jesus laying hands of healing on the multitude who implored him for salvation from disease and crippling, and Jesus bringing salvation to all by accepting the agony and shame of crucifixion. The dark side of the Christmas story is much closer to its bright side in the Nephite story.

And this same close connection between the bright and the dark—between glory and suffering—continued as other Book of Mormon prophets added other elements to the Christmas story. Samuel the Lamanite painted a breathtaking and awesome picture of a day, a night, and a day without darkness—truly a season of glory as a sign of Christ's birth. But almost in the same breath, Samuel continued with the sign of Christ's death—a terrible time of intense darkness and destruction so violent that it would rend the very rocks of the earth.

What connects these two halves of the Christmas story—the birth and the death followed by resurrection? We do. Our hearts are the bridge over which the Christmas story comes. Samuel the Lamanite told the Nephites that his prophetic mission from God was to "cry unto this people, Repent and prepare the way of the Lord." (Helaman 14:9.) What is the way of the Lord? It is our hearts, offered to him in repentance and hope and faith.

The Christmas story is a story about faith. The Christmas

story seems very real to us. We can recognize the nativity scene at a glance. We can immediately identify the woman, the man, the child. We understand what the setting is. And on at least some level, part of us thinks, "If I'd been there in Bethlehem, I'd have known. I would have recognized Joseph and Mary. I would have known who this baby is."

I hope that's true. I hope it's true for you and I hope it's true for me. But the fact of the matter is that hundreds of people in Bethlehem and Egypt and later still in Nazareth saw Mary and Joseph and Jesus and still didn't know who that baby was or who his mother was.

The shepherds recognized who this baby was because they had seen the angel with the eye of faith and heard the glorious angel choir with the ear of faith.

The wise men recognized who this baby was because they had looked upon the star with the eye of faith.

But it wasn't until John the Baptist looked upon Jesus with the eye of faith that he saw the Lamb of God who would take away the sins of the world. (See 1 Nephi 10:10.) It wasn't until Simon and Andrew looked upon Jesus with the eye of faith that they saw someone who could make them fishers of men. (See Matthew 4:18–20.) Even though Peter walked on water and cast out devils and stood on the Mount of Transfiguration, it wasn't until he looked upon Jesus with the eye of faith that he could say, "Thou art the Christ, the Son of the living God." (Matthew 16:16.)

There are beautiful and glorious places in our lives, and there are dark and destructive places in our lives, just as there are in the Christmas story. The way of Jesus is to go into both places, to make the glorious places even more radiant, to bring wholeness to the broken places, and to transform the dark places into light. But he can only go on the way that we offer willingly to him. He can only pass through the gates that we open to him. He can only make whole the broken fragments that we put into his hands. He is the newness of the baby in the manger and the eternality of Christ the Redeemer who created the heavens and the earth. He tells us, as he told the Nephites:

> As many as have received me, to them have I given to become the sons [and daughters] of God; and even so will I to as many as shall believe on my name, for behold, by me redemption cometh. . . .
>
> I am the light and the life of the world. I am Alpha and Omega, the beginning and the end. (3 Nephi 9:17–18.)

The Christmas story begins with a baby, but it does not end there. It continues through a ministry of healing and holiness. It continues through sacrifice and suffering. It continues through resurrection and redemption. It will never end until we accept Christ's grace and mercy. Our Christmas story will never end until we lay hold on the loving invitation of the Savior: "If ye will come unto me ye shall have eternal life. Behold, mine arm of mercy is extended towards you, and whosoever will come, him will I receive; and blessed are those who come unto me." (3 Nephi 9:14.)

We are blessed beyond the Nephites in having the tenderness, the wonder, the beauty, and the joy of the Christmas story in Bethlehem. We are blessed beyond the Israelites of Palestine in having the clarity, the strength, the urgency, and the power of the Christmas story that the Nephites had—in understanding as they understood that pain and joy are intermingled, that rejoicing and suffering run together, that beyond the cradle is the cross and beyond both is the glory of the risen Savior who conquered the anguish of death and the deeper anguish of sin for us. This year, as we celebrate and rejoice in and relish every detail of the Christmas story, let's remember the baby, but let's also remember the man who was healer and teacher. Let's remember the infant, but let's also remember the son of God who did his Father's will to give us eternal life.

He has told us:

> Ye shall offer for a sacrifice unto me a broken heart and a contrite spirit. And whoso cometh unto me with a broken heart and a contrite spirit, him will I baptize with fire and with the Holy Ghost. . . .
>
> Behold, I have come unto the world to bring redemption unto the world, to save the world from sin.
>
> Therefore, whoso repenteth and cometh unto me as a little child, him will I receive, for of such is the kingdom of God. Behold, for such I have laid down my life, and have taken it up again; therefore repent, and come unto me ye ends of the earth, and be saved. (3 Nephi 9:20–22.)

This Christmas may we become as little children, that we may fully accept and understand and rejoice in the Babe of Bethlehem and these blessings.

5

SHEPHERDS ABIDING

Someone once said there are three periods in a person's life:

1. When you believe in Santa Claus.
2. When you don't believe in Santa Claus.
3. When you are Santa Claus.[1]

Well, we're all at stage 3. We are Santa Claus. And sometimes it seems like we are dragging the whole sleigh by ourselves, if you know what I mean. A lot of times Christmas is not a happy, carefree time for women, especially not for Mormon women who have many children involved in many activities and who are also involved in busy neighborhood, church, and community activities on their own. Sometimes we just need to lighten up and focus on the basics, the way children do. Here are some glimpses into what we might call the basics of Christmas:

When the teacher asked the class, "Why was Jesus born in Bethlehem?" a boy raised his hand and replied, "Because his mother was there."[2]

A Sunday School teacher asked her class why Joseph and Mary took Jesus with them to Jerusalem. "They couldn't get a babysitter," a small child replied."[3]

A Sunday School teacher was telling her class of fourth-graders the Christmas story about the three wise men bringing gifts to the baby Jesus. A little girl who had recently become the big sister of a brand-new baby brother said, "Well, I guess gold and all that stuff are all right, but I'll bet Mary really wished somebody had brought some diapers."[4]

Does any of this sound familiar? Baby-sitters, and where mom is, and diapers. It's all part of the wonderful, mysterious season of Christmas that can break your heart or break it open so that you see and experience new things. So let's begin with one of the old, old stories about Christmas—the story of the shepherds. Let's review the story of the shepherds found in Luke chapter 2.

> And there were in the same country shepherds abiding in the field, keeping watch over their flock by night.
> And, lo, the angel of the Lord came upon them, and the glory of the Lord shone round about them: and they were sore afraid.
> And the angel said unto them, Fear not: for, behold, I

bring you good tidings of great joy, which shall be to all people.

For unto you is born this day in the city of David a Saviour, which is Christ the Lord.

And this shall be a sign unto you; Ye shall find the babe wrapped in swaddling clothes, lying in a manger.

And suddenly there was with the angel a multitude of the heavenly host praising God, and saying,

Glory to God in the highest, and on earth peace, good will toward men.

And it came to pass, as the angels were gone away from them into heaven, the shepherds said one to another, Let us now go even unto Bethlehem, and see this thing which is come to pass, which the Lord hath made known unto us.

And they came with haste, and found Mary, and Joseph, and the babe lying in a manger.

And when they had seen it, they made known abroad the saying which was told them concerning this child.

And all they that heard it wondered at those things which were told them by the shepherds.

But Mary kept all these things, and pondered them in her heart.

And the shepherds returned, glorifying and praising God for all the things that they had heard and seen, as it was told unto them. (Luke 2:8–20.)

I want to draw my message from just two words: "shepherds abiding." There were shepherds abiding in the field, keeping watch over their flocks by night. I want to explore with you three aspects of what it means for us as Mormon men and women to be shepherds abiding, particularly at Christmastime. First, I want to talk about abiding in the field, and what some of those fields might be. Second, I want to talk about abiding in faith. And third, I want to talk about abiding in the Savior's love.

I think that *abide* is a beautiful word. Unlike many words in English that come to us from Latin or French or Greek, this word is an English word, *abidan*. It has endured almost unchanged for hundreds of years since Old English, from the time of the earliest documents in A.D. 700 until about 1100. It has always had two meanings: one is to stay, to continue, to wait patiently; and the second meaning is to endure unchanged. *Abide* is a woman's word; it is a home word. So much of what we have to do is to endure, to be consistent, to rest unchanging, to wait, to stay, to dwell, to remain.

Abiding is not a flashy or a glamorous quality; it does not make a lot of noise or cause a lot of upheaval. But at the same time, it is not a passive quality. Abiding takes tenacity and integrity and a strong awareness of the power of choice. It's the verb that the Apostle Paul chose when he talked about the most important qualities we could have as believers: "And now abideth faith, hope, charity, these three; but the greatest of these is charity." (1 Corinthians 13:13.) Think of the triumph that it represents to say, "And now abideth faith. And now abideth hope. And now abideth charity." After the turmoil and shouting and temptations and trials and turbulence, what a victory to say, "And now abideth Deborah. And now abideth Lois. And now abideth Maria."

91

Abiding in the Field

So let's talk about shepherds abiding in the field. When we talk about this scripture, we usually talk about the faithfulness of the shepherds. They were out in the field by night taking care of their sheep. Well, I want to stress that they were where they were supposed to be. They were in the field. The angels knew where to find them. At the appointed time, in the appointed place, the shepherds were where they belonged and, as a result, they heard the song of praise and joy that had been prepared from the beginning of the world.

The shepherds were doing their job. They were doing their work. Because Christmas is a time when our normal work goes on and when a lot of extra work happens, let's talk about work. "Work" sounds like one of the four-letter words that make us tired just thinking about it. "Duty" is another one of those four-letter words. So are the words "task" and "jobs." They don't sound fun. They don't sound like a vacation. They don't sound like a holiday. But I don't think most of us are so out of touch with reality that we think a holiday just happens without a lot of hard work on somebody's part. And in a family, that someone is usually the mother. So let's talk about work.

You can probably all relate to the person who said, "The world is full of willing people—some willing to work, the rest willing to let them."[5] Most of us have forgotten that the original meaning of *holiday* was *holy day,* although Christmas comes as close as any day of remembrance of combining the two concepts. Rabbi Harold Kushner gave me some insights into the nature of work as holiday when he said:

When work is done in the right frame of mind, [it] can be holy. There is a linguistic connection between the words "work" and "worship." Work can be a way of serving God. Whatever we do for a living, we can learn to see it not only for the money we earn, but in terms of the blessings and benefits it brings other people. My colleague Rabbi Jeffrey Salkin has written a book, *Being God's Partner*, about a spiritual approach to our work. In it, he describes a man who works for a moving-van company and brings a religious approach to his work. The man explains that moving is stressful for most people. They are unsure about what awaits them in their new community. When he makes the experience of packing and shipping their belongings a pleasant, stress-free one by his attitude, when he speaks to them of the new opportunities which are theirs, he believes he is serving God by making those people less fearful.

Rabbi Salkin [also] writes of a lingerie saleswoman who sanctifies her otherwise ordinary job by being especially sensitive and compassionate to the mastectomy patients who come to her store. When our son-in-law completed his orthodontic training at Boston University's dental school, he invited me to say a few words to his classmates at their graduation party. I told them, "When people ask you, 'What do you do?' don't tell them, 'I'm an orthodontist,' or 'I put braces on people's teeth.' Tell them, 'I help people have beautiful smiles and feel good about themselves.' It will not only be good for business; it will help you feel good about your work."[6]

What is your work? Not only does everything Rabbi Kushner said about careers and paid employment apply, but wives and mothers are also engaged in an enormously important and holy work. It is the same work that God himself is engaged in—to bring to pass the immortality and eternal life of human beings by learning about God ourselves, by exemplifying the principles in our lives about what it means to be a human being who knows God, and by teaching others, in our own families and in other circles, what it means to know God by the radiance of our own faith and the immense gratitude of our own love for God.

This may sound like those sappy Mother's Day sermons that sentimentalize and also trivialize motherhood by presenting it as a shining moment under plastic wrap, untouched by human hands. Well, I'm talking about reality—reality with peanut butter smudges on it and missing socks and sulky teenagers. We're talking about work—mother-work, elbow-grease work, unsung, unpraised, usually unnoticed W-O-R-K! And I'm saying, "Abide." Abide the peanut butter and the socks and sulks. Do your job. Stay in your field. Don't abandon our sheep, even when it's cold and dark, because that's when the angels come, and the silence is when you hear the angel voices. What is your field? Where are you called to abide? This Christmas, can you abide there, in faith and hope and charity?

Now, perhaps your work is different—no mother-work or career work but a calling of the heart. With the shepherd's attitude, abide in that field. I want to tell you about a woman named Diane who suffers from multiple sclerosis. She has to be fed everything, pushed everywhere in a wheelchair. Her fingers are curled and rigid. Her voice is barely a whisper. She can do hardly anything for herself. Her life is about as limited as a life can be. "[People] would look at Diane—stiff and motionless—and shake their heads. . . . People might look at her and say, 'What a shame. Her life has no meaning. She can't really do anything.'" But Diane has a rich and meaningful life because of her work; she is a warrior of prayer. She has a corkboard on the wall by her bed with rows of photographs and names on it. Each of the names is someone she prays for, every single day.

She moves mountains that block the paths of missionaries.

She helps open the eyes of the spiritually blind in southeast Asia.

She pushes back the kingdom of darkness that blackens the alleys and streets of the gangs in east L.A.

She aids the homeless mothers . . . single parents . . . abused children . . . despondent teenagers . . . handicapped boys . . . and dying and forgotten old people in the nursing home down the street where she lives.

Diane is on the front lines, advancing the gospel of Christ, holding up weak saints, inspiring doubting believers, energizing other prayer warriors, and delighting her Lord and Savior.

This meek and quiet woman sees her place in the world. . . . [She] is confident, convinced her life is significant. Her labor of prayer counts. . . . Whether you sit at a typewriter, behind the wheel of a bus, at the desk in a classroom, in a chair by your kitchen table, or [lie] in bed and pray, [your] life is hidden with Christ. You enrich His inheritance. You are His ambassador. In Him your life has depth and meaning and purpose, no matter what you do.

Someone has said, "The point of this life . . . is to become the person God can love perfectly, to satisfy His thirst to love."[7]

Diane abides. She is a shepherd, abiding in her field, even when her field is no larger than her bed and her wheelchair.

I hope we can all feel the strength of abiding in our fields, even when they seem cold and dark. Let's be where we are supposed to be so that angels can find us. Let's be in our meetings. Let's be about doing service. Let's be where people need us. Let's be in our homes with our families.

Abiding in Faith

Now, let's talk about the second point relative to abiding. And by this I mean abiding in faith that doing our duty and doing our jobs is important work, even when it's not glamorous or spectacular. The prophet Malachi asked a very searching question: "Who may abide the day of his coming? And who shall stand when he appeareth?" This is a text that Handel selected for one of his beautiful solos in the *Messiah* about the coming of the Lord. Malachi continues, "The Lord, whom ye seek, shall suddenly come to his temple, even the messenger of the covenant, whom ye delight in: behold, he shall come, saith the Lord of hosts." (Malachi 3:1–2.)

We are called by those who bear the message of the covenant to become covenant-makers and covenant-keepers ourselves, so that we will be prepared when the Lord comes suddenly to his temple. I am not talking only about his literal return to usher in the Millennium and his reign of peace upon this troubled earth of ours, but I am also talking about the return that each one of us can experience as we literally "prepare him room," in the words of that beautiful Christmas carol "Joy to the World." How can we abide the day of his coming if we cannot abide the moments and hours of his coming? Why would we want to be in his presence forever if we do not want to be in his presence today, this hour?

The Doctrine and Covenants records the answer to Malachi's question as bestowed by the Lord upon the Saints of our own day. The Lord told Joseph Smith that "mine own elect . . . will hear my voice, and shall see me, and shall not be asleep, and shall abide the day of my coming; for they shall be purified, even as I am pure." (D&C 35:20–21.)

We can abide the day of the Savior's second coming when we can abide his coming today—for he longs to be with us. He is not withholding his presence from us to punish us or tease us or teach us to be patient. He is just waiting for an invitation from a heart prepared to make him room. When Jesus was baptized, "John bare record, saying, I saw the Spirit descending from heaven like a dove, and it abode upon him." (John 1:32.) There's that word again—*abode*. The Spirit made its dwelling place, its abode with the Savior. But that is exactly the promise we all received as we emerged from the waters of baptism. One having authority laid his hands upon our heads and spoke the words that are both a commandment and an invitation: "Receive the

Holy Ghost." If we will, the Holy Ghost will abide with us, a guest more permanent than a parent or a spouse, a visitor more familiar than the faces of our children.

For our part, abiding in faith means that we accept that promise wholeheartedly, that we do our part to prepare him room. Ruth Somers has written a lovely poem on this theme:

> *"Would you like to hold the baby?"*
> *The gentle Mary might have said*
> *To the shepherds who were kneeling*
> *By her Holy Infant's bed.*
>
> *"Would you like to hold the baby?"*
> *She might have asked those men of old,*
> *Three wise men who had offered Him*
> *Myrrh, frankincense, and gold.*
>
> *"Would you like to hold the baby?"*
> *She might ask of us today,*
> *"Hold the blessed Christmas spirit*
> *Deep within your hearts to stay?"*[8]

We must have faith in good and goodness even in the presence of evil. We must have faith in light, even in the presence of darkness. We must believe in the power of the Christ-child even in the presence of Herod's soldiers.

I want to tell you a Christmas story about a test of that faith. The Bennett family of Crawfordville, Georgia, celebrated Christmas as a family, beginning with their six children and seventeen grandchildren living in homes scattered over their eight-acre property. It started with an outdoor set of nativity figures that lit up. They strung lights. People on the road stopped when they heard the family caroling and joined them for displays, strung a few more lights, and hand-lettered scriptures on plywood panels to explain the Christmas story. They called it Christmas in Dixie.

The mother, Lyda Jean, discovered an unexpected talent for soft-sculpture, and they added other scenes: a lamplighter, a Christmas guest, Frosty the Snowman, and a hay wagon full of "folks going home for Christmas, a military camp scene to honor the troops overseas." By their tenth year, 1992, they had about 50,000 visitors and 75,000 lights. Visitors roasted 19,000 hot dogs, and Lyda served 2,718 gallons of hot chocolate. But then horrible things happened. Teenagers pulled down strings of lights, pried open the gingerbread house, and knocked over the horses pulling the hay wagon. Two weeks before Christmas, vandals sneaked in and trashed the place. They slashed the stuffed animals, tore off baby Jesus' head, and threw him in the mud. They tipped over other scenes and tossed the other figures around. On the morning the children came running in with this terrible news, Lyda Jean wrote:

> It was as if a family member had died. My insides collapsed and my heart could hardly beat. We had spent all our time and money, and we had never asked for anything in return except for people to enjoy themselves. The blood was pulsating in my head. I wondered how the world had come to the awful point where just for meanness people would sneak on our place and tear up everything we had done to make a nice Christmas for the community.

But she was not prepared for the outpouring of community support. A self-described "hardnosed bachelor," in tears, pulled out a hundred dollar bill and handed it to her. A neighbor with a pickup began gathering the decorations that had been strewn for five miles down the road. People sewed the sculptures back together, brushed off the mud, and set up the displays.

By Monday morning a radio station had started collecting donations. Firefighters from nearby Richmond County organized volunteers and donations of decorations. But the thing that touched me the most was the phone calls. As soon as I hung up, the phone rang again. A pilot said, "Mrs. Bennett, I've never been to your place, but when I fly over it, that's the warmest feeling in the world, and I know I'm home safe once again."

A lady said, "If you don't fix anything else, make sure the soldier scene goes back up. My son was in Desert Storm, and he had never seen his baby. We took pictures of the baby at the military camp display and sent them to him, and that was the first look he got at his baby."

A woman from South Carolina called. "My husband and I had been coming every year. Last year we were going to get a divorce. It was a sad Christmas, but I decided I would take my little girl over to you anyway. When we arrived, lo and behold, there was my husband. We decided to make another go of it, and now we're happier than we've ever been."

I must have had a hundred callers that Monday, each one with a tale to tell of how much Christmas in Dixie had meant to them. That night I thought, *Well, Sunday was the worst day of my life, and now today has been the best.*

On Tuesday, with the help of the firefighters and all the volunteers we could use, we glued, patched, wired and sewed everything back together. It wasn't one hundred percent but it was good enough. As I sewed the head back on baby Jesus and put him in the manger, I remembered something that happened the first year we had done the manger scene. A blind lady in her eighties named Alice was brought over one evening. I took her hand, read her the scriptures on the board and then described each scene. When we got to the manger, she let go of my hand and went in, hugged the figures and called out in prayer, "Oh, Lord! Oh, Jesus!"

Some 50 people watched her reverently. I thought, Those figures are only fabric, stuffing and paint—just material things. But don't tell Alice that. Because right now she's hugging baby Jesus.

[Then Lyda Jean thought,] Now, as I laid [the baby] back in the manger, I figured the vandals had miscalculated. They too thought that what we had was just boards and lights and material. But I learned that it was more. It was a place where families came back together, where the lonely found a spot by the fire, where people from institutions felt normal, where a rich lady in a fur coat could stand next to a dirty, runny-nosed little boy roasting a hot dog.

This was where the story of baby Jesus could make Christmas real again, where spiritual awakenings could take place. I've got to tell you, I know. Because my own tired and torn-up spirits had been warmed up pretty good. And it was Christmas in Dixie again.[9]

I don't know what burdens you're carrying at this season of the year. Perhaps some of them can be lifted and perhaps some of them can only be lightened, and for still others you will have to pray for strength as you abide them in patience and endurance. But please, abide in faith and let that faith strengthen and speak to you.

Abiding in the Savior's Love

And now I want to share with you some thoughts about the love of the Savior and abiding in his love. This is a time for singing Christmas carols, but instead I would like to remind you of the words of a hymn, one that is a prayer that expresses the yearning and hope of our heart and yet, at the same time, our faith in the promise of our Savior to always be with us that we may abide in his love.

> *Abide with me! Fast falls the eventide;*
> *The darkness deepens. Lord, with me abide!*
> *When other helpers fail and comforts flee,*
> *Help of the helpless, oh, abide with me!*
>
> *Swift to its close ebbs out life's little day.*
> *Earth's joys grow dim; its glories pass away.*
> *Change and decay in all around I see;*
> *O thou who changest not, abide with me!*
>
> *I need thy presence ev'ry passing hour.*
> *What but thy grace can foil the tempter's pow'r?*
> *Who, like thyself, my guide and stay can be?*
> *Thru cloud and sunshine, Lord, abide with me!*[10]

I want to bear testimony to the Savior's love. Think what it means that Jesus told his apostles and, through them, us, in this glorious gospel:

> Abide in me, and I in you. As the branch cannot bear fruit of itself, except it abide in the vine; no more can ye, except ye abide in me.
>
> I am the vine, ye are the branches: He that abideth in me, and I in him, the same bringeth forth much fruit: for without me ye can do nothing. . . .
>
> If ye abide in me, and my words abide in you, ye shall ask what ye will, and it shall be done unto you. . . .
>
> As the Father hath loved me, so have I loved you: continue ye in my love.
>
> If ye keep my commandments, ye shall abide in my love; even as I have kept my Father's commandments, and abide in his love. (John 15:4-5, 7, 9-10.)

We have talked about difficulties of abiding—the hard times, the lonely times, the enduring times. But this scripture is about a sweet time, a time of complete trust and acceptance when we abide in the Savior's love just as if that love were our dwelling place, our home where our heart can safely rest.

> I grew up believing that Christmas was a time when strange and wonderful things happened, when wise and royal visitors came riding, when at midnight the barnyard animals talked to one another, and in the light of a fabulous star God came down to us as a little Child. Christmas to me has always been a time of enchantment, and never more so than the year that my son Marty was eight.

That was the year that my children and I moved into a cozy trailer home in a forested area just outside of Redmond, Washington. As the holiday approached, our spirits were light, not to be dampened even by the winter rains that swept down Puget Sound to douse our home and make our floors muddy.

Throughout that December, Marty had been the most spirited, and busiest, of us all. He was my youngest, a cheerful boy, blond-haired and playful, with a quaint habit of looking up at you and cocking his head like a puppy when you talked to him. Actually, the reason for this was that Marty was deaf in his left ear, but it was a condition that he never complained about.

For weeks I had been watching Marty. I knew that something was going on with him that he was not telling me about. I saw how eagerly he made his bed, took out the trash, and carefully set the table and helped Rick and Pam prepare dinner before I got home from work. I saw how he silently collected his tiny allowance and tucked it away, spending not a cent of it. I had no idea what all this quiet activity was about, but I suspected that somehow it had something to do with Kenny.

Kenny was Marty's friend, and ever since they had found each other in the springtime, they were seldom apart. If you called to one, you got them both. Their world was in the meadow, a horse pasture broken by a small winding stream, where the boys caught frogs and snakes, where they would search for arrowheads or hidden treasure, or where they would spend an afternoon feeding peanuts to the squirrels.

Times were hard for our little family, and we had to do some scrimping to get by. With my job as a meat wrapper and with a lot of ingenuity around the trailer, we managed to have elegance on a shoestring. But not Kenny's family. They were desperately poor, and his mother was having a real struggle to feed and clothe her two children. They were a good, solid family. But Kenny's mom was a proud woman, very proud, and she had strict rules.

How we worked, as we did each year, to make our home festive for the holiday! Ours was a handcrafted Christmas of gifts hidden away and ornaments strung about the place.

Marty and Kenny would sometimes sit still at the table long enough to help make cornucopias or weave little baskets for the tree. But then, in a flash, one would whisper to the other, and they would be out the door and sliding cautiously under the electric fence into the horse pasture that separated our home from Kenny's.

One night shortly before Christmas, when my hands were deep in Peppernoder dough, shaping tiny nutlike Danish cookies heavily spiced with cinnamon, Marty came to me and said in a tone mixed with pleasure and pride, "Mom, I've bought Kenny a Christmas present. Want to see it?" So that's what he's been up to, I said to myself. "It's something he's wanted for a long, long time, Mom."

After carefully wiping his hands on a dish towel, he pulled from his pocket a small box. Lifting the lid, I gazed at the pocket compass that my son had been saving all those allowances to buy. A little compass to point an eight-year-old adventurer through the woods.

"It's a lovely gift, Martin," I said, but even as I spoke, a disturbing thought came to mind. I knew how Kenny's mother felt about their poverty. They could barely afford to exchange gifts among themselves, and giving presents to others was out of the question. I was sure that Kenny's proud mother would not permit her son to receive something he could not return in kind.

Gently, carefully, I talked over the problem with Marty. He understood what I was saying.

"I know, Mom, I know!." . . . But what if it was a secret? What if they never found out who gave it?"

I didn't know how to answer him. I just didn't know.

The day before Christmas was rainy and cold and gray. The three kids and I all but fell over one another as we elbowed our way about our little home putting finishing touches on Christmas secrets and preparing for family and friends who would be dropping by.

Night settled in. The rain continued. I looked out the window over the sink and felt an odd sadness. How mundane the rain seemed for a Christmas Eve! Would wise and royal men come riding on such a night? I doubted it. It seemed to me that strange and wonderful things happened only on clear nights, nights when one could at least see a star in the heavens.

I turned from the window, and as I checked on the ham and lefse bread warming in the oven, I saw Marty slip out the door. He wore his coat over his pajamas, and he clutched a tiny, colorfully wrapped box in his pocket.

Down through the soggy pasture he went, then a quick slide under the electric fence and across the yard to Kenny's house. Up the steps on tiptoe, shoes squishing;

open the screen door just a crack; place the gift on the doorstep, then a deep breath, a reach for the doorbell, and a press on it hard.

Quickly Marty turned, ran down the steps and across the yard in a wild race to get away unnoticed. Then, suddenly, he banged into the electric fence.

The shock sent him reeling. He lay stunned on the wet ground. His body quivered and he gasped for breath. Then slowly, weakly, confused and frightened, he began the grueling trip back home.

"Marty," we cried as he stumbled through the door, "what happened?"

His lower lip quivered, his eyes brimmed. "I forgot about the fence, and it knocked me down!"

I hugged his muddy little body to me. He was still dazed, and there was a red mark beginning to blister on his face from his mouth to his ear. Quickly I treated the blister and, with a warm cup of cocoa soothing him, Marty's bright spirits returned. I tucked him into bed and just before he fell asleep he looked up at me and said, "Mom, Kenny didn't see me. I'm sure he didn't see me."

That Christmas Eve I went to bed unhappy and puzzled. It seemed such a cruel thing to happen to a little boy while on the purest kind of Christmas mission, doing what the Lord wants us all to do—giving to others—and giving in secret at that. I did not sleep well that night. Somewhere deep inside I must have been feeling the disappointment that the night of Christmas had come and it had been just an ordinary, problem-filled night, no mysterious enchantment at all.

But I was wrong.

By morning the rain had stopped and the sun shone. The streak on Marty's face was very red, but I could tell that the burn was not serious. We opened our presents, and soon, not unexpectedly, Kenny was knocking on the door, eager to show Marty his new compass and tell about the mystery of its arrival. It was plain that Kenny didn't suspect Marty at all, and while the two of them talked, Marty just smiled and smiled.

Then I noticed that while the two boys were comparing their Christmases, nodding and gesturing and chattering away, Marty was not cocking his head. When Kenny was talking, Marty seemed to be listening with his deaf ear. Weeks later a report came from the school nurse, verifying what Marty and I already knew. "Marty now has complete hearing in both ears."

The mystery of how Marty regained his hearing, and still has it, remains just that—a mystery. Doctors suspect, of course, that the shock from the electric fence was somehow responsible. Perhaps so. Whatever the reason, I just remain thankful to God for the good exchange of gifts that was made that night.

So you see, strange and wonderful things still happen on the night of our Lord's birth. And one does not have to have a clear night, either, to follow a fabulous star."

Conclusion

This Christmas season let us think of the shepherds abiding in the field, but let us also think of the angels who found them there, doing their jobs. Let us think about the holiness of work that is done with a consecrated attitude. Think about our need to abide in faith even in the presence of evil, and remember Lyda Jean Bennett's family, making Christmas in Dixie. And above all, remember the Savior's promise that we can abide in his love and experience the richness and fullness of the life that he lives because he will give us that same life.

May our Savior abide with us, and may the promised Spirit we received at our confirmation abide with us and in us and shine through us, that the angels who find us keeping watch in our fields will recognize some of their own light and glory in us.

NOTES

1. Rev. James A. Simpson, as quoted in *Holy Humor*, edited by Cal and Rose Samara (Carmel, Calif.: Guideposts, 1996), 205.

2. Rev. William Armstrong, S.J., as quoted in *Holy Humor*, edited by Cal and Rose Samara (Carmel, Calif.: Guideposts, 1996), 202, adapted.

3. Catherine Hall, in ibid., 202.

4. Jim McDonough, as quoted in ibid., 202–3.

5. *God's Little Devotional Book for Leaders*, compiled by W. B. Freeman Concepts, Inc. (Tulsa, Okla.: Honor Books, 1997), 130.

6. Harold S. Kushner, *How Good Do We Have to Be?* (Boston, Mass.: Little, Brown and Company, 1996), 147–48.

7. Joni Eareckson Tada, "Significance," *Stories for the Heart*, compiled by Alice Gray (Sisters, Oreg.: Multnomah Books, 1996), 230–31.

8. Ruth Somers, "Would You?" *Christmas Classics* (booklet), (no publisher, no date), not paginated.

9. Lyda Jean Bennett, "Christmas in Dixie," *Guideposts*, December 1995, 2–6.

10. *Hymns* (Salt Lake City: The Church of Jesus Christ of Latter-day Saints, 1985), no. 166.

11. Diane Rayner, "An Exchange of Gifts," *The Best Stories from Guideposts* (Wheaton, Ill.: Tyndale House Publishers, 1987), 219–22.

6

CHRISTMAS EXTRAVAGANCE

I've titled this chapter *"Christmas Extravagance"* because Christmas seems to be a time of delicious, glorious abundance, profusion, and excess—a real cornucopia of a time. I realized I felt this way about it as I listened to one of those presentations I'm sure we've all heard—about how you have to deal with the stress of the holidays by setting priorities, establishing limits, making yes-lists and no-lists, deciding what you'll eat and what you won't, working out a budget, a schedule, a plan. It all sounded very prudent, moderate, controlled, restrained. It all sounded very boring. It sounded like no fun at all.

Yet I realized that it made good sense, and I know that the Christmas season is ruined for some people by bingeing—they spend too much, eat too much, do too much, and run too fast and too hard. They end up feeling sad, selfish, and sinful. So how could I actually want extravagance? Isn't that awfully reckless and foolish of me?

I began thinking about where this idea of mine might have come from, and I realized it comes from thirty-three years in elementary school. Sometimes we complain that Christmas seems to start in the middle of November. Well, in elementary school, Christmas actually starts the week before Halloween. Remember that second-grade feeling when you got to magically transform your identity into that of a fairy princess or a cowboy and go out after dark to the homes of perfect strangers and chant some strange words like "Trick or treat" and they would pour candy into your bag? If that's not plenitude, what is? And the grown-ups who are always saying "We can't afford it" or "You haven't earned it" or "Have you been a good girl or boy?" aren't asking any of those questions. They're just smiling at you and laughing with you and praising your magic wand or your furry chaps and dishing out the candy some more. Do you remember that second-grade feeling?

And then comes Thanksgiving, which has something to do with people in funny hats carrying guns with bell-shaped muzzles and turkeys and Indians and America but mostly being very thankful and grateful for all our blessings and going over the river and through the woods to Grandmother's house.

And then comes Christmas, the red-and-green holiday, with trees and strings of popcorn and the incredibly delicious power of knowing that you're making a present for your mom and dad and it's your secret and they don't even know about it because you're doing it at school. And there are treats and Santa Claus and Christmas carols and people making wishes like "Merry Christmas," and that's magic too, like "Trick or treat" but somehow even better.

And you don't find out about it at school, but there's a baby—baby Jesus—who is an important part of Christmas, and a stable with a donkey with furry ears and a cow with gentle eyes, and the wise men in splendid costumes with the glamorous camels, and Mary and Joseph and the shepherds holding lambs and wonderful crooks. But they're all looking at the baby, and on their faces is an expression that makes you feel a little funny inside. It's a peaceful, thoughtful expression that brings stillness, even in the midst of the blinking lights and the ho-ho-ho's and the "Merry Christmases." And so you look at the baby too, and a little of the stillness comes into your own heart. And somehow you remember the baby, even while the presents get deeper under the tree and some of them have *your* name on them, and you help your mom make the gingerbread house, and you get to make shingles on the roof out of those nasty pink wafers that you wouldn't touch at any other time of the year, but somehow they taste like Christmas.

And so I have to tell you that I have a very second-grade approach to Christmas. It's the culmination of three important months in a child's life that start with an experience of transformation into someone special and an outpouring of grace—candy, not because you've earned it but just because you are—and then continue with a linking of hardship and thankfulness and culminate at the darkest time of the year in a festival of lights, music, singing, and jolly Santas with more gifts. And that baby. Don't forget that baby.

So I'm not very sympathetic with the yes-lists and the no-lists. And it's not just because they don't sound very much like fun. It's because they don't sound very much like joy. If it's true that you can never get enough of what you don't need, then maybe it's also true that you can never give too much of what you have in plenty.

Let's think about extravagance for Christmas. Think about the plenteousness of Christmas—its abundance, copiousness, liberality, bounty, lavishness, exuberance, luxuriance, profusiveness; its unstinted, unmeasured, inexhaustible plenty. What can we be extravagant with? What do we have in abundance?

Let me name a few things just to get you started. We all have an absolutely unlimited supply of smiles. Sometimes we save them just for the family. Or worse, sometimes we save them just for the people at work. Well, they are *not* in short supply! Let's start passing them out, one per every pair of eyes we look into, with a few left over so that we can catch ourselves smiling even when we're alone.

Something else that we've all got in unlimited abundance is a supply of greetings. "Merry Christmas!" If you think about it, it's a wonderful greeting. It's not just the marker of a day or a season; it's also a profound wish for a certain quality, that this day or this season will be marked by the quality of a merry heart, one so full of happiness that it spills over into laughter and delight. Every time you wish someone a "Merry Christmas," it's like a personal vote for that person's delight and happiness.

You also have an unlimited fountain of song springing up. Don't you just thrill to the exuberance and beauty of Christmas carols? It's fun and easy to sing at Christmastime. Every radio, every department store, every supermarket fills the air with seasonal songs. You may not like all of them, but you have good feelings about most of them because they are, after all, connected to Christmas, that time of superabundance. A song weighs nothing and takes up absolutely no storage space. It sounds better if you sing it out loud, but it doesn't mind singing away all by itself in your heart while you're on a crowded elevator or sitting in the world's slowest-moving meeting. It improves immeasurably if you sing it with someone else, especially a child, and it doesn't matter where it ends—even in the middle of the third verse when you can't remember what line comes next—as long as you laugh about it.

Now, I happen to think that Christmas music fits any time of the year. I really enjoy requesting "Far, Far Away on Judea's Plains" as a rest song when I go out on assignments—not only because I enjoy the song but also because I enjoy the startled looks on people's faces when I ask for this song in the middle of August. But I also think that one of the most wonderful things about singing at Christmas is that all music seems to fit the season. If you want to sing "Jingle Bells," that's great. If you want to sing "Shine On, Harvest Moon," that's a reminder about the bounties the Lord has blessed us with. If you want to sing "Popcorn Popping on the Apricot Tree," it's a signal of the hope we have in Christ. I think it *all* fits.

But some of the most beautiful Christian music ever written

was written for this season of the year. One of the new songs I learned as an adult—and it's not a traditional carol at all—is called "'Twas in the Moon of Winter Time." It was written to the tune of an old French carol during the early seventeenth century by Father Jean de Brebeuf. Father de Brebeuf was a Jesuit missionary who worked among the Huron Indians in Canada (he died in 1649), and he wrote this carol to tell the story of baby Jesus to them in a language and with images they could understand.

This carol is extremely meaningful to me because, as a Japanese Buddhist, I always experienced Christmas as a borrowed holiday. There are no Japanese Christmas carols. There are no Buddhist Christmas carols. But for people like me, the many mansions of the gospel have open doors to accept us in our diversity and to welcome us in and give us a place at the table and a present under the tree. I cannot think of Christmas without thinking of the many people who generously translated the holiday into terms that I could understand, first as a little Buddhist girl, then as a shy new convert trying to understand Mormonism, then as a Hawaiian transplanted to Utah with its snow and lighted street decorations. I do not know Father de Brebeuf, but I am thankful in my heart to him for rewriting the Christmas story into Huron to open the doors of that miracle time to them. Because of his act of compassion, he has the honor of having written the first Canadian Christmas carol and perhaps the first carol in the New World.[1]

> *'Twas in the moon of wintertime when all the*
> *leaves had fled*

The mighty Gitchee Manitou sent angel choirs
*   instead.*
Before their light the stars grew dim,
And wandering hunters heard the hymn:
Jesus, your king, is born. Jesus is born.
In excelsis gloria!
The earliest moon of wintertime was not so round
*   and fair*
As was the ring of glory on the helpless infant
*   there.*
While chiefs from far before him knelt,
With gifts of fox and beaver pelt.
Jesus, your king, is born. Jesus is born.
In excelsis gloria!
O children of the forest free, O sons of Manitou,
The holy child of earth and heaven is born this day
*   for you.*
Come kneel before the radiant boy,
Who brings you beauty, peace and joy,
Jesus, your king, is born. Jesus is born.
In excelsis gloria!

This song makes me think of the scripture, "For behold, the Lord doth grant unto all nations, of their own nation and tongue, to teach his word, yea, in wisdom, all that he seeth fit that they should have." (Alma 29:8.)

Let's look at what else you have to give for Christmas. You have time. Even though you may think that time is what you have in shortest supply, you have all the time there is, all the time in the world, the morning and the evening, the day that God has made for us to rejoice and be glad in. Think of it not as a machine to be used for maximum efficiency but as a gift to be given with open hands and an open heart.

You also have an unlimited number of prayers to offer during this season. You can pray for the people in the hospital as you drive by. You can pray for the policeman directing traffic after the basketball game. You can pray for the person you see on the news whose face and plight touch you, even if you see her face only in a crowd. You can pray for the clerk in the shoe store, for the Salvation Army bell ringer, for the grandchild in Florida, for the president of the United States, for the person standing in the detergent aisle trying to make up her mind what soap to buy. And this doesn't even begin to touch the hundreds of people you know personally for whom you can pray.

Think of the power of that prayer. It's as if you lift someone with loving hands and hold him or her up in remembrance before God. That person is in your memory, in your heart, in your thoughts. And now you have brought his or her name before God in joyous, sympathetic remembrance. What a wonderful gift of plenitude!

Now, perhaps you're thinking, "But some of these people are strangers. I don't even know them. I don't know if they need my prayers. I don't know if my prayers will do them any good." That's not the point. You're not praying for them because *they* need it. You're praying for them because *you* have a prayer to give. The prayer does not exist because of their poverty; it exists because of your richness.

And think what it means that *you* have this inexhaustible

treasury of benevolence and bounty. Why, it means that you're rich, wealthy, overflowing with abundance! You can lavish it, squander it. It doesn't matter. You can never give so much that you'll run out.

Think of the Christmas story. Isn't one of the things we love about it the absolute feast or famine that characterizes it? Mary and Joseph were not only poor but homeless, not only away from their families but thrown totally on the mercy of strangers. These are extreme circumstances—extravagantly bad circumstances. The visitors who came to see the Christ child were not moderately well-off, moderately respectable, or cautiously optimistic. They were the extremes of society—poor shepherds and gorgeously appareled kings bearing fabulous gifts. The shepherds did not take a vote, arrange a sheep-watching schedule, and come to the stable when it was light enough to walk comfortably on the road. They left their flocks and came with haste in the darkness of night. God did not send a neatly typed heavenly memo to the religious and theological leaders of the day, but a multitude of angels filled the sky and the night with their song of glory and rejoicing.

Do you have faith that you can give to someone? That someone may feel that God is far away. But remember, you are not giving the gift because he or she needs it but because you have it to give.

Do you have a compliment to give someone out of your treasurehouse of appreciation? Do you have forgiveness to give out of your own rich sense of the Father's endless mercy?

Did you get ideas from President Howard W. Hunter's 1994 Christmas devotional speech about your richness? He said:

> This Christmas, mend a quarrel. Seek out a forgotten friend. Dismiss suspicion and replace it with trust. Write a letter. Give a soft answer. Encourage youth. Manifest your loyalty in word and deed. Keep a promise. Forgo a grudge. Forgive an enemy. Apologize. Try to understand. Examine your demands on others. Think first of someone else. Be kind. Be gentle. Laugh a little more. Express your gratitude. Welcome a stranger. Gladden the heart of a child. Take pleasure in the beauty and wonder of the earth. Speak your love and then speak it again. Christmas is a celebration, and there is no celebration that compares with the realization of its true meaning—with the sudden stirring of the heart that has extended itself unselfishly in the things that matter most.[2]

What do you have to give? The keys to God's storehouse are in your hands. You are richer than Midas. Think about your abundance! What extravagant gift can you give this Christmas out of your bounty?

"Give," said Jesus, "and it shall be given unto you; good measure, pressed down, and shaken together, and running over." (Luke 6:38.) And how did Jesus give? Listen to what Paul says, and to how extravagantly he says it:

> God loveth a cheerful giver.
> And God is able to make all grace abound toward you; that ye, always having all sufficiency in all things, may abound to every good work:

(As it is written, He hath dispersed abroad; he hath given to the poor: his righteousness remaineth for ever.

Now he that ministereth seed to the sower both minister bread for your food, and multiply your seed sown, and increase the fruits of your righteousness;)

Being enriched in every thing to all bountifulness, which causeth through us thanksgiving to God.

For the administration of this service not only supplieth the want of the saints, but is abundant also by many thanksgivings unto God . . . for the exceeding grace of God in you.

Thanks be unto God for his unspeakable gift. (2 Corinthians 9:7–12, 14–15.)

You are the heir of eternity. All that the Father hath is yours. Can his storehouse ever be empty? There is no scarcity or rationing or restriction. When he pours out blessings, he opens the windows of heaven, and we cannot contain what he showers upon us. We are infinitely precious to him, infinitely loved, infinitely cherished. You can never give away too much of what cannot be exhausted in you—the inexhaustible, unstinted love of God.

I pray for all of us the merry heart that comes with Merry Christmas, the cheerful giving that God loves, the overflowing faith, the plenitude of hope, and an eternity of charity.

NOTES

1. Commentary accompanying "'Twas in the Moon of Wintertime," Pamela Conn Beall and Susan Hagen Nipp, *Wee Sing for Christmas* (Los Angeles: Price/Stern/Sloan, 1985), 24–25.
2. As quoted in Lynn Arave, "Keep True Holiday Spirit, LDS Leaders Counsel," *Deseret News,* 5–6 December 1994, B-1.

7

TWO OR THREE FOR CHRISTMAS

No matter how old we are or how young we start, there's always something new to learn about Christmas. Those who have three-year-olds in their extended family can relate to this story. A little boy was going to be a shepherd in his nursery school Christmas pageant. He could hardly wait for his costume; but when his mom tried it on him, he was completely confused. Looking up at her "with perplexed eyes he asked, 'You mean I don't get to be a German shepherd?'"[1]

Encounters with One or Two

I'd like to talk about a scripture we don't often associate with Christmas. This is the promise that Jesus gave his disciples: "Where two or three are gathered together in my name, there am I in the midst of them." (Matthew 18:20.) This promise was important enough that the Savior renewed it when he was speaking to the Saints in our own dispensation: "I say unto you, as I said unto my disciples, where two or three are gathered together in my name, as touching one thing, behold, there will I be in the midst of them—even so am I in the midst of you." (D&C 6:32.)

We think of Christmas as a time for sharing, a time for being surrounded by our families, a time for rejoicing with our wards and stakes, a time for celebrating with our friends, a time for sending Christmas cards that express our shared happiness to distant loved ones, and a time for reaching out to strangers. But I want to look at the ways in which the Christmas story was an application of these scriptures.

Think of the many prophets who saw and foretold the coming of the Savior: Isaiah seeing in vision the virgin who would bear a son "and shall call his name Immanuel." (Isaiah 7:14.) Think of Nephi seeing a young mother "most beautiful and fair above all other virgins . . . bearing a child in her arms." (1 Nephi 11:15, 20.) Each man was alone, reaching across the immensity of time and space through the witness of the Holy Ghost, to recognize and salute that young woman and worship the child in her arms. Do you think that perhaps Mary also knew, somehow, through the intermediary of that same Spirit, that men she had never seen in the flesh and who had died hundreds of years before she was born were loving her and wishing her well and blessing her for her willingness to give birth to the Savior? Surely, our Lord was there with those two or three who were gathered together in his name.

And think of Mary's first direct intimation of her mission,

when the Angel Gabriel appeared to her and blessed her in the name of the Most High and promised her that her son would "reign over the house of Jacob for ever; and of his kingdom there shall be no end." (Luke 1:33.) The two of them were alone together. It wasn't a meeting. It wasn't a public ceremony. There were no witnesses. But surely the Savior was there with them, loving this young woman who would offer her body as the vessel through which he could be born into his mission in mortality. Surely where those two were gathered, there he was with them.

And think of the next events of the Christmas story. When Mary journeyed to see her cousin Elisabeth, the two women were apparently alone when they met, but in the most intimate and sacred of all ways, they were a gathering of four. Elisabeth cherished within herself the growing body of her baby son, who would become the prophet, John the Baptist. And Mary cherished within her body as well the little body that Jesus Christ, the Savior of the world, would inhabit while he was in mortality. Jesus was literally in their midst, and they knew it by the operation of the Holy Ghost that made John the Baptist leap for joy in Elisabeth's womb. Somehow, it communicated instantly to Elisabeth that this was not just the random or normal movement of the growing child but a salutation of great significance between a future prophet and his Lord. Surely Mary was speaking the truth when she said, "My soul doth magnify the Lord, and my spirit hath rejoiced in God my Saviour." (Luke 1:46–47.) An eternity of prophecy and an eternity of redemption were meeting in that one mortal moment, and surely there was our Savior in the midst of that moment.

Think of the next event: Joseph realized, troubled, that this lovely young woman who was his betrothed wife was already with child. He had an encounter in a night vision or dream with the angel who reassured him that he should not fear to take Mary as his wife, for her child was "of the Holy Ghost" and would "save his people from their sins." (Matthew 1:20–21.) Joseph and the angel were alone, but surely a third person was also present. Surely Jesus Christ was there, filled with love and gratitude for this simple carpenter who would protect his mother; become, to all intents and purposes in the eyes of the people, Jesus' own father; and whose children by Mary would become the brothers and sisters in Jesus' immediate family. Were there ever moments later in their family life when the veil was so thin between this almost-father and almost-son that they remembered that encounter in a dream of the night? I wonder.

Think of the shepherds who came by night to the stable in Bethlehem with the song of the angels ringing in their ears. Even tradition does not assign a number to the shepherds, but I suspect they were not a large group. And I wonder if there was a moment when they looked into Jesus' eyes and the Spirit bore witness to each one of them, as if each was alone with the child, that here was the Son of God. I think perhaps they did know, because they returned to their flocks "glorifying and praising God for all the things that they had heard and seen, as it was told unto them." (Luke 2:20.)

Think of the wise men who came a few weeks or a few months later. We don't know how many there were—more than one, certainly. Tradition says there were three, but we don't know, nor do we know where they came from, how long they were on the road, and how they could interpret the star that no one else seems to have noticed. It was another holy moment when Jesus, as a child, was literally in their midst, but also when the Holy Ghost testified that he was the Savior of the world. We know this happened because the wise men "worshipped him" (Matthew 2:11), and yet the townspeople of Bethlehem among whom Mary and Joseph were living then apparently did not see anything remarkable or extraordinary about this little baby born to the couple from Nazareth. Jesus was in *their* midst, too, but they didn't recognize him.

Or think of the presentation in the temple. That great and beautiful building was thronged with people, those buying and selling, those presenting their offerings, priests busily officiating in their callings. Jesus was in their midst too, as his parents fulfilled the sacrifice required for a firstborn son, but only two people recognized him out of that great multitude.

The first was Simeon, who was led "by the Spirit into the temple" and took Jesus in his arms. He "blessed God, and said, Lord, now lettest thou thy servant depart in peace . . . for mine eyes have seen thy salvation." (Luke 2:27–30.)

The second was the prophetess Anna, who was also led by the Spirit, for the record says she came "in that instant," saw the baby, and recognized in him the longed-for "redemption" of the people and "gave thanks likewise unto the Lord." (Luke 2:38.)

Think of those encounters: Joseph, Mary, the baby, and two faithful, aged persons, whose moment of recognition was the reward of a lifetime of faithfulness.

Do you think that Jesus, as he grew up, remembered this encounter that occurred when he was a baby? Or that possibly Joseph and Mary told him about them and he struggled to make sense of them and fit them with his growing awareness of his mission? Or that possibly the Spirit reached through the veil to him to make that meaning clear to him? After all, everything we know about Jesus' ministry could be described as either the recognition or the nonrecognition of those around him. What made the difference in those who saw him with their spiritual eyes as well as their physical eyes and saw in him their salvation? What made the difference for those who saw him with curiosity or contempt or even hatred so that they desired to kill him?

Consider again Jesus' promise to his disciples: "Where two or three are gathered together in my name, there am I in the midst of them." (Matthew 18:20.) That phrase—"gathered together in my name"—is an important one. I think there are some promises that those who had Jesus present in their midst in the flesh could not claim because they were not willing to be there "in his name."

And this, of course, raises the question that I want us to ponder: Are the gatherings we participate in, whether with a single person or with many, are these gatherings in the name of Jesus so that we can claim his promise to be there in our midst? I hope so. It's a promise Jesus offered graciously, offered willingly, offered eagerly. He wants us to claim it. He wants to be with us, hallowing and sanctifying the feeling that we should have for each other as brothers and sisters on this earth.

In thinking about that question, I'd like to recall the words to "It Came upon the Midnight Clear." When I was in Kirtland, Ohio, and by the courtesy of the Community of Christ, which owns and so beautifully maintains the Kirtland Temple, the singles conference I was meeting with was allowed to meet in that beautiful structure. In the Community of Christ hymnal is a verse for "It Came upon the Midnight Clear" that I'd never seen as part of this song before, and I found it to be so beautiful that I would like to share it.

> *O ye, beneath life's crushing load,*
> *Whose forms are bending low,*
> *Who toil along the climbing way*
> *With painful steps and slow!*
> *Lo now, for glad and golden hours*
> *Come swiftly on the wing.*
> *O rest beside the weary road,*
> *And hear the angels sing.*[2]

Our Stories of the One and Two

I'd like to share four stories that illustrate the willingness of the Savior to be in a gathering, however spontaneous and brief, that takes place in his name.

You probably know of Norman Vincent Peale, a wonderful minister of another faith who has given thousands of people hope and encouragement by reminding them that the message of the gospel is truly the good news. It was a lesson that he himself had to learn as a boy. He grew up in Cincinnati, Ohio, where his father, a former physician, was a minister. One Christmas Eve, when he was about twelve, he was shopping with his father. It was cold. He was tired and a little grumpy. He writes:

> I was thinking how good it would be to get home, when a beggar—a bleary-eyed, unshaven, dirty old man— came up to me, touched my arm with a hand like a claw, and asked for money. He was so repulsive that instinctively I recoiled. Softly my father said, "Norman, it's Christmas Eve. You shouldn't treat a man that way."
>
> . . . "Dad," I complained, "he's nothing but a bum."
>
> "But he's still a child of God," my father said.
>
> He then handed me a dollar—a lot of money for those days and certainly for a preacher's income. "I want you to take this and give it to that man," he said. "Speak to him respectfully. Tell him you are giving it to him in Christ's name."
>
> "Oh, Dad," I protested, "I can't do anything like that."
>
> My father's voice was firm. "Go and do as I tell you."
>
> So, reluctant and resisting, I ran after the old man and said, "Excuse me, sir. I give you this money in the name of Christ."
>
> He stared at the dollar bill, then looked at me in utter amazement. A wonderful smile came to his face, a smile so full of life and beauty that I forgot that he was dirty and unshaven. . . . Graciously he said, "And I thank you, young sir, in the name of Christ."
>
> All my irritation, all my annoyance faded away. The street, the houses, everything around me suddenly seemed beautiful because I had been part of a miracle that I have seen many times since—the transformation that comes

over people when you think of them as children of God, when you offer them love in the name of a Baby born two thousand years ago in a stable in Bethlehem, a Person who still lives and walks with us and makes His presence known.[3]

This story is about two encounters: Norman and his father, and that young boy and the old shabby man. And don't you think our Savior was in their midst too? I certainly do.

In the second story, Norman's father received a telephone call from the madam of a house of ill repute, saying that one of the girls in the house was dying and calling for a minister. Would he come? Without hesitating, Norman's father said he would, then told Norman to come along. His mother was shocked. She didn't want her son in such a place! But Norman's father said:

> "There's a lot of sin and sadness and despair in human life. Norman can't be shielded from it forever."
>
> We walked through the snowy streets and I remember how the Christmas trees glowed and winked in darkness. We came to the . . . big old frame house. A woman opened the door and led us to an upstairs room. There, lying in a big brass bed, was a pathetic, almost doll-like young girl, so white and frail that she seemed like a child, scarcely older than I was.
>
> Before he became a minister, my father had been a physician and he knew the girl was gravely ill. When he sat by her bed, the girl reached for his hand. She whispered that she had come from a good Christian home. . . . She

said she knew she was dying and that she was afraid. "I've been so bad," she said. "So bad."

I stood by my father's side listening. I didn't know what anybody could do to help her. But my father knew. He put both his big strong hands around her small one. He said, "There is no such thing as a bad girl. There are good girls who act badly sometimes, but there are no bad girls—or bad boys either—because God made them and He makes all things good. Do you believe in Jesus?" The girl nodded. He continued, "Then let me hear you say, 'Dear Jesus, forgive me for my sins.'" She repeated those words. "Now," he said, "God loves you, His child, and He has forgiven you, and no matter when the time comes, He will take you to your heavenly home."

If I live to be a hundred [wrote Norman] I will never forget the feeling of power and glory that came into that room as my father prayed for that dying girl. There were tears on the faces of the other women standing there, and on my own, too. And everything corrupt, was simply swept away. Actually there *was* beauty in that place of evil. The love born in Bethlehem was revealing itself again in a dark and dismal house . . . and nothing could withstand it. It seemed to wash all evil from human hearts.[4]

Norman says that there was beauty in that awful place where women sold their bodies. How could that be possible? Because the Savior was in their midst, with that dying girl, with Norman, with his father, and with the women who were tending that girl in her last illness.

Think of your own circumstances. Maybe your holidays will

be crammed to the brim with wall-to-wall children, grandchildren, friends, and neighbors; caroling at a rest home; taking meals to shut-ins; and running the third-grade Christmas party and the ward Christmas party. Remember that each one of those gatherings, no matter whether it lasts three seconds or a whole evening, is a gathering into which you can invite the Savior and which he will be eager and overjoyed to attend.

And maybe for you, even though you will be busy, there will be moments of solitude, perhaps even of loneliness. They needn't be lonely. I think that even the act of writing a Christmas card and thinking with love of the person you will be sending it to as you stick on the stamp is a little gathering of two into which you can invite the Savior, and surely, surely he will be there in your midst.

I had a Christmas moment late one year. After an incredibly long, hot summer, I was thirsty for snow, longing for the cool refreshment and the promise of water. But that first snowstorm came while I was out of town, and when I got back, I could barely drive into my garage. The wind had blown the snow all over my front deck until I couldn't even get the door open. Furthermore, it had thawed and then frozen again so that there was a hard crust of snow and ice sticking to the deck with the rest of the snow on top. I thought, "Oh, no! What can an island girl do with all of *this* on her front step?"

So I did the sensible thing. I picked up the phone, dialed a number, and called, "Bishop! Help!"

He said, "I'll be right there." And the next thing I knew, there was my bishop, Melvin Young, doing hand-to-hand combat with the ice and drifted snow while I sprinkled salt and swept off the loose stuff. I don't think he stopped smiling the entire time—and it was hard work. I was afraid his teeth would freeze.

When he was all finished and I was thanking him, he said, "Chieko, I would do anything in the world for you."

I knew he was telling me the truth, not because I'm so lovable but because he's so loving. He would do anything in the world for me because he'd do anything in the world for any member of the ward. He truly loves us all and loves his calling because it's an opportunity to serve. And I love him.

There were just two of us on that cold, front deck in the snow, but the Savior was on the deck with us. We were two of three, gathered together in a moment of love and service, and the Savior was in our midst.

In conclusion, I want to share another story. It's a story with a sad and even a terrible setting, but one in which there are radiant moments of love and joy. It's a Christmas story when the gift was the scriptures, and I'm telling it to you because Christmas is a time when the scriptures assume a new preciousness, an urgent value.

This story is told by James E. Ray, an American prisoner in Vietnam in 1966. He had been shot down while he was flying a mission in May 1966 and captured, interrogated, and tortured many, many times. Now he was imprisoned alone in a tiny cell with only a damp pallet for a bed. He would not be released for five long, terrible years, years of inadequate food, physical suffering, inadequate clothing, no contact with the outside world. Where would you turn for strength?

On this particular day, when he was wishing he'd gone down with the plane, he heard a whisper. He writes:

> I heard it again. An unmistakable, "Hey, buddy?"
>
> I scrambled flat on the floor and peered through the crack under the door. I could see I was in one of many cells facing a narrow, walled courtyard. The whisper had come from the next cell. I whispered back. . . . We waited as the guard passed and then began to converse.
>
> Soon all the prisoners on that yard were whispering. We started by learning about one another, where we were from, our families. One day I asked Bob what church he went to.
>
> "Catholic," he said. "And you?"
>
> "Baptist."
>
> Bob was quiet for a moment, as if my mention of church evoked deep memories. Then he asked, "Do you know any Bible verses?"
>
> "Well, I know the Lord's Prayer," I answered.
>
> "Everyone knows that."
>
> "How about the Twenty-third Psalm?"
>
> . . . I began whispering it. He repeated each line after me. A little later he whispered back the entire psalm.
>
> Other prisoners joined in, sharing verses they knew. . . .
>
> As the number of prisoners grew, two of us shared a cell. My first cellmate was Larry Chelsey, a Mormon from Idaho. Though we had a few differences of belief, our common denominators were the Bible and Jesus Christ, and we were able to share and write down a great deal of

scripture. It became vital to our daily existence. Often racked with dysentery, weakened by the diet of rice, thin cabbage, and pumpkin soup, our physical lives had shrunk within the prison walls. We spent 20 hours a day locked in our cells. And those Bible verses became rays of light, constant assurances of God's love and care.

We made ink from brick dust and water or precious drops of medicine. We wrote verses on bits of toilet paper and slipped them to others, dropping them behind a loose brick at the toilets.

It was dangerous to do that. . . . A man unlucky enough to be caught passing a note would be forced to stand with his arms up against a wall for several days, without sleep.

. . . One night I lay with my ear pressed against the rough wooden wall of my cell to hear thump . . . thumpety-thump as somewhere, cells away, a fellow POW tapped out in Morse code: "I will lift up mine eyes unto the hills, from whence cometh my help." (Psalm 121:1.)

He . . . passed on the seven other verses in that psalm, which I scratched on the concrete floor with a piece of broken tile. "My help cometh from the Lord," the psalm assured us, and with that assurance came his presence, soothing us, telling us not to fear.

By 1968, more of us were squeezed together and for two years four of us lived in an eight-by-eight foot cell. . . . Only by following Christ's teachings about constant forgiveness, patience, and understanding were we able to get along together. . . .

Two and a half years went by before I could write Dad

and Mother. A year later I was allowed to receive my first letter. In the meantime we subsisted on letters written nearly 2000 years before.

By the early 1970s, almost all of the American POWs had been moved to . . . the main prison in downtown Hanoi. . . . Some 50 of us lived, ate and slept in one large room. . . . We were surprised to find how many of the men knew scripture, learned from those verses passed along in whispers, on toilet paper and through wall thumpings. We immediately made plans for a Christmas service. A committee was formed and we started to work.

Green and red thread decorated the walls, a piece of green cloth was draped like a tree. Our crèche was made of figures carved from soap or molded from papier-mâché of moistened toilet paper.

We pooled the verses we knew and made a . . . Bible, written covertly on scraps of paper. . . . The reader began: "In those days a decree went out from Caesar Augustus that all the world should be enrolled . . ." As he completed this verse, a six-man choir sang "O Little Town of Bethlehem."

He went on: "And she gave birth to her first-born son. . . ." "Away in a manger, no crib for his bed . . ." sang the choir.

. . . With eyes shining and tears trickling through beards, we joined in the singing. Glinting in the light of the kerosene lamp was a cross made from silver foil.

Occasionally the guards knocked on the door, ordering us not to sing, but they finally gave up. Our program continued into a Communion service led by . . . a Lutheran

. . . as Episcopalians, Methodists and men of other denominations bowed their heads.

A Jewish prisoner . . . entertained us by singing "the eight days of Hanukkah" to the tune of "The Twelve Days of Christmas." Amid the laughing and singing, we looked up to find the prison commander and interrogators watching.

Later that night, after many months of our asking, the commander brought us a real Bible, the first any of us had seen in prison. He said we could keep it for one hour. We made the best of it. . . .

[After] several months [of] . . . continual requests, one of us was allowed to go out and copy from it for one hour each week.

But when we started to copy, the interrogator planted his elbow on the Bible for the first 15 minutes. Then, after letting us start, he asked mundane questions to distract us. I just ignored him and wrote as fast as I could. The next week we had to return the previous week's copy work. They seemed afraid for us to keep the scriptures, as if they sensed the spiritual help kept us from breaking.

From that we learned a most important lesson: Bible verses on paper aren't one iota as useful as scriptures burned into your mind, where you can draw on them for guidance and comfort.

After five weeks we didn't see the Bible again. But that had been enough time for us to memorize collectively the Sermon on the Mount, Romans 12, First Corinthians 13, and many of the psalms. Now we had our own "living

Bible" walking around the room. By this time we had Sunday worship services and Sunday School classes. . . .

Two years passed this way . . . years of continuing degradation, sickness, hunger and never knowing whether we would see home again. But instead of going mad or becoming animal-like, we continued to grow as a community, sustaining one another in compassion and understanding.

For as one of the verses I heard thumped out on the wall one night said: "Man doth not live by bread only, but by every word that proceedeth out of the mouth of the Lord." (Deuteronomy 8:3.)[5]

Can you imagine how eagerly and with what love the Savior was in the midst of these hungry, homesick men who revered his word and shaped their lives according to the precepts of his precious word? Think about it the next time you pick up your own copy of the scriptures.

Conclusion

Remember the promise that Jesus gave his disciples: "Where two or three are gathered together in my name, there am I in the midst of them." (Matthew 18:20.)

Jesus began fulfilling this promise even before he gave it to his apostles. He fulfilled it, I believe, when the Angel Gabriel appeared to the lovely young woman who became his mother, and in that sacred gathering of two women and two unborn infants when Mary visited her cousin Elisabeth. I believe that he was there when Joseph agreed to fulfill the marriage and become the Lord's foster father. And of course, at his birth, he came literally into their midst and was there for the visit of the shepherds and again for the visit of the wise men.

I believe that the Savior is in our midst, in any gathering characterized by love and kindness and service. He was there when young Norman Peale handed his father's hard-earned dollar to the tramp and when his father comforted a young woman who was dying after a life of sin. I believe that the Savior was on my front deck when my bishop showed up with his smile and his shovel. And I know he was in that Hanoi prison as a group of hungry, sick Americans gathered to share the spiritual strength of the scriptures.

We have the scriptures. We have the Savior's promise. We have each other. And surely, surely, he will be in the midst of us as we gather together, whether in a planned meeting or an encounter that lasts only a few seconds, if we do it in the name of a Christian and carrying his spirit of love and service and kindness.

NOTES

1. Joan Banks, "Canine Confusion," in *Life in Our House* (Bloomington, Minn.: Garborg's Heart 'n Home, 1994), December 19.
2. Edward H. Sears, "It Came Upon the Midnight Clear," *Hymns of the Saints* (Independence, Mo.: Herald House, 1981), no. 256.
3. Norman Vincent Peal, *The Positive Principle Today* (Avenel, N.J.: Wings Books, 1992), 292–95.
4. Ibid.
5. James E. Ray, "The Secret of Our Survival," *Guideposts*, January 1996, 10–13.